THE
MILK-FREE AND
MILK/EGG-FREE
COOKBOOK

THE
MILK-FREE AND
MILK/EGG-FREE
COOKBOOK

by
Isobel S. Sainsbury, M.D.

With a Foreword by
Jerome Glaser, M.D.

ARCO PUBLISHING, INC.
NEW YORK

First Arco Edition, Second Printing, 1980

Published by Arco Publishing, Inc.
219 Park Avenue South, New York, N.Y. 10003

Library of Congress Cataloging in Publication Data

Sainsbury, Isobel S
  The milk-free and milk/egg-free cookbook.

  Includes index.
  1. Cookery for allergics.   I. Title.
RM221.A6S24   1979   641.5'63   78-18364
ISBN 0-668-04693-7 (Library Edition)
ISBN 0-668-04701-1 (Paper Edition)

Printed in the United States of America

INTRODUCTION

TWENTY YEARS AGO with the arrival of my third child, I was introduced to the need for milk-free and milk-free, egg-free recipes. Over the years, I have sought and collected these, altered old family ones, and developed a few original ones. I have put together this collection for other families whose members must have dietary restrictions as far as milk or milk and eggs are concerned. You will notice that I say members, for it is my experience that the rest of the family may take milk in some form, but they are served the milk-free cookies and cakes and casseroles of the dieter. From the beginning my recipes had to pass the criticism of the older children, father, mother and grandmother of our dieter. If I failed to win their approval I would have been forced to cook two meals at once. Since I never had that kind of time, I had to find recipes to please everyone—I hope they will please the readers, too.

In preparing this cookbook we have tried to indicate which recipes are milk-free and which are milk-free, egg-free; but it is better to read through the recipe before preparing it, for some contain other common allergens you may or may not be able to use such as nuts or chocolate. Since my son was not limited on these, they are included. Recipes have been included which give you a chance to enlarge your menus especially on holidays, birthdays, parties, etc.

What are the basics for a milk-free diet? Some foods are very simple and easy to buy and prepare. For example, here is a menu sample:

Breakfast: Juice or fruit

Cereal—white sugar and hot water, or milk or cream substitute if desired

Toast—of milk-free bread spread with milk-free margarine or honey, jam or cinnamon and sugar

Bacon or sausage

Lunch: Chicken rice soup
                Sandwich of milk-free bread and filling as described
                    in the sandwich chapter
                Fruit —plain or in gelatin

Dinner: Meat—pot roast
                Potato—boiled, baked, French fried
                Vegetable—plain
                Salad—tossed salad with Italian dressing
                Dessert—Banana Freeze

    What happens to this basic diet when the milk-free dieter
travels away from home?

Breakfast: Fruit juice
                Cereal—sugar and hot water (milk and cream substi-
                    tute are not available in restaurants)
                (no toast, rolls or muffins can be found marked milk-
                    free)
                Bacon or sausage
                sometimes JellO® is available

Lunch: Soup—be careful, the only milk-free one you can be
                    sure of is chicken rice or chicken pastina or beef
                    bouillion or consommé
                Sandwich—order a meat that is not blended, i.e. don't
                    order bologna. Instead order ham, chicken, tur-
                    key, beef or hamburger, but do not eat the roll.
                Order rye bread with no butter.
                Potato chips
                Salad—tossed salad with dressing
                Fruit or JellO plain—beware of whipped cream on
                    top

Dinner: Meat (no casserole or Italian dishes)
                Potato—boiled, French fried or baked (if they don't
                    open it in the kitchen to add butter before you
                    get it.)
                Vegetables—better to omit, usually you can't count
                    on their being butter-free

Salad—tossed or green

Dessert—best to skip this and have something you brought along such as a cookie in your room later.

It is the variety that is so limited when you eat away from home. Parties are another difficulty. For my child I was always able to speak to the hostess and provide his food. As an adult this isn't so easy, so he simply refrains from eating any but the obvious milk-free foods. Don't trust another person's cooking to be free of milk—*ASK*.

As far as shopping is concerned one develops (one *has* to develop) the fine print habit. Read the ingredients and then re-read the ingredients. Watch Out for *Milk, Non-Fat Milk, Milk Protein, Casein* and *Sodium Caseinate,* and *Whey, Dried Milk Solids.* These are all milk in one form or another. If the product is not labeled, *don't* buy it. Watch food labeled "Non-Dairy," many are not.

Many companies will gladly provide you with lists of their milk-free products if you wish to take a moment to write to them requesting such. Some of them will also send recipes. A few of these that I have found most cooperative are:

For milk-free products:

Keebler Co., 100 Keebler Square, Medford, Oregon 97501

Kannengiesser and Co., Inc., 96 Ninth Ave., New York, New York 10010

General Foods Kitchens, 250 North St., White Plains, New York 10602

Kraft Products

Arnold

A & P

National Biscuit Co.

For recipes:

Syntex Laboratories, Inc., Palo Alto, California 94304

Ross Laboratories, 625 Cleveland Ave., Colombia, Ohio 43216

Mead Johnson and Co., Evansville, Indiana 47721

Loma Linda Foods, Medical Products Division, Riverside, California 92505

Rich Products Corp., 1145 Niagara St., Buffalo, New York 14213—Coffee Rich®

Best Foods, Division Comm. Products Co., 10 East 56th St., New York, New York

Presto Food Products Inc., 1101 East 16th St., Kansas City, Missouri 64108—Mocha Mix

Once again I stress the need to read the *ingredients* in the fine print on the product before you buy for a milk-free product. Perseverance counts—don't omit—look.

FOREWORD

THE RECORDED HISTORY of cow's milk as a food for man goes back at least six thousand years. Despite this, the cow, who so rightly deserves the title of Foster Mother of the Human Race, after thousands of years of domestication still makes milk immunologically designed for calves and not for human beings. It is because of this that cow's milk may cause allergic reactions in man. Cow's milk, unless the infant is fed breast milk (which does not of itself cause allergic reactions), is commonly the first food given to an infant and at an age when the defenses against allergy are not fully developed. This is the reason that allergy to cow's milk is the most common form of allergy to food in the human being. Cow's milk is, nevertheless, for the individual with whom it agrees, the greatest gift of food that nature has given to mankind. Next to cow's milk, eggs are the most common cause of food allergy, and it is because of this that a booklet designed to help individuals allergic to milk and eggs is particularly appropriate.

Since the problem of getting along without these foods may be very difficult, expert advice, such as is given in this book, is highly essential. The author, an exceedingly capable practicing physician, has had considerable experience with the dietary management of allergic disease, not only in her own family, where her son was the most food allergic patient I have ever encountered, but with food allergies in many of her patients. She writes with intimate firsthand knowledge of the problem, and this book will, I am sure, afford much desired help and comfort in the management of the individual who cannot tolerate either or both of these foods.

JEROME GLASER, M.D.

CONTENTS

THE MILK-FREE AND
MILK/EGG-FREE COOKBOOK

CHAPTER 1
BREADS, BISCUITS AND PANCAKES

I T IS POSSIBLE TO BUY, on the market, many commercially made milk-free breads. *Read* the ingredients and the fine print. If none is listed, do *not* use. Remember that *sodium caseinate* and *whey* are milk products. Most rye bread, many Italian and French breads, and some whole wheat breads contain no milk, so watch for them.

For this reason, only a very few bread recipes are included.

Milk-Free
Egg-Free

Biscuits

Hard-to-find, milk-free dough can be used for many things such as shortcake, rolls, meat pies, etc.

> 2 c. cake flour or 1¾c. bread flour
> 2 tsp. baking powder
> 1 tbsp. sugar
> ¾ c. cream substitute
> 1¼ tsp. salt
> 3 tbsp. milk-free margarine

Sift together flour, baking powder, salt and sugar. Cut into the flour mixture with two knives or a pastry blender the milk-free margarine. Add the cream substitute by making a well in the middle of the above. Mix slowly. When absorbed, stir vigorously until dough leaves sides of bowl. Use as drop biscuits on top of meat or fruit mixtures.

OR:

Turn the dough onto a lightly floured board. Knead it gently for

$\frac{1}{2}$ minute. Roll to $\frac{1}{4}$ to $\frac{1}{2}$ width thickness. Cut with floured biscuit cutter. Brush tops with milk-substitute or milk-free margarine. Pick up with spatula and bake on a greased cookie sheet at 425° until done (about twelve minutes).

Mother's Date-Nut Bread

Great! Rich!

2 c. dates, ground
1 tbsp. melted shortening
1 egg
2 tsp. soda
1 tsp. vanilla
1½ c. boiling water
1 c. light brown or white sugar
2½ c. flour
½ tsp. salt

Mix dates, pour boiling water over them, and let stand for twenty minutes. Then add shortening, sugar, egg, flour, soda, salt and vanilla. Line bread pan with wax paper. Bake one hour at 325°-400°

Banana Bread

Very Popular

2 c. bread flour
¼ tsp. soda
¾ c. sugar
1 egg, beaten well
3 tbsp. Coffee Rich
½ tsp. baking powder
¼ tsp. salt
¼ c. milk-free margarine
2/3 c. mashed banana
½ c. nuts optional

Sift together flour, baking powder, soda and salt. Blend sugar and milk-free margarine until light. Add egg and banana. Add Coffee Rich. Alternate in three parts with the flour mixture. Nut meats may be added if desired. Bake in 8 x 4-inch loaf pan at 350° for one hour.

Banana Muffins*

2 well-ripened bananas, mashed
1/3 c. white sugar
¼ c. oil or milk-free margarine
½ tsp. vanilla
½ tsp. baking soda
2 tsp. baking powder
1¼ c. rice flour
¼ tsp. salt

Mix bananas, sugar and oil or milk-free margarine. Add and mix baking powder, vanilla, rice flour, baking soda and salt. Turn into greased muffin tins or a small loaf pan. Bake at 325° for 25 minutes for muffins and ¾ hour for loaf.

Ice Box Rolls

2/3 c. sugar
2 eggs
6 tbsp. milk-free margarine
10 c. flour (measured after sifting)
2 cakes compressed yeast in ½ c. lukewarm water
1 tsp. salt
2 c. boiling water

Dissolve sugar, salt and shortening in boiling water. Dissolve yeast in lukewarm water. Allow sugar mixture to cool, then add yeast. Sift in flour a little at a time until you have added 1 cup, then add well-beaten eggs and rest of flour as soon as this thickens. Chill, let rise, and bake.

---

*Reprinted with permission from Allergy Information Association, Weston, Ontario, Canada.

Rich Griddle Cakes*

3 c. flour
1 tsp. salt
1 egg
2 tbsp. melted milk-free margarine
1½ tsp. baking powder
¼ c. sugar
2 c. milk substitute

Mix batter and bake as directed. *(For variation add 1 cup blueberries.)*

To Bake Griddle Cakes:
Heat a griddle or skillet and test temperature by sprinkling with a few drops of water. If water disappears at once, the griddle is too hot. If it flattens out and boils, the griddle is not hot enough. If the drops bounce, the griddle is ready for use. Brush lightly with fat, using a pastry brush. Pour batter in uniform amounts from a pitcher or from tip of a large spoon. When cakes are full of bubbles turn with a pancake turner and brown other side. Turn only once.

Plain Waffles*

2 c. flour
2 tbsp. sugar
2 eggs, separated
4-6 tbsp. melted butter (milk-free margarine)
2 tsp. baking powder
½ tsp. salt
2 c. milk substitute

Sift dry ingredients twice. Beat egg whites until stiff but not dry. Set aside. Beat egg yolks, add milk substitute, and mix with dry ingredients only enough to blend them. Add milk-free margarine. Fold in the beaten egg whites last. Bake in electric waffle iron. Serve with any syrup or sauce. Makes 6 waffles.

These recipes may be baked ahead and frozen and heated in toaster when desired.

Pancakes for Small Family

1 tsp. melted milk-free shortening
1 c. Coffee Rich or non-dairy creamer
1 c. cake flour
½ tsp. soda
1 egg
½ tsp. vinegar
¾ c. regular flour
½ tsp. salt

Combine shortening, coffee rich and vinegar. Sift together cake flour, regular flour, soda and salt. Lightly beat one egg. Combine and bake in hot griddle. Double recipe if necessary for more than three people. This recipe may also be made ahead, frozen, and individually heated in the toaster. This works well for a quick breakfast.

French Toast

2 eggs
2/3 c. milk substitute
6 slices day-old, milk-free bread
½ tsp. salt
milk-free margarine

Beat eggs lightly, with salt and milk substitute. Dip bread into mixture, fry on both sides in hot butter (milk-free). Or bake dipped toast on buttered pan at 500° until top browns: turn, continue to bake until brown on other side. Serve with maple syrup, blueberry syrup, or any syrup or use milk-free butter and powdered sugar or spread with jam.

Orange Nut Bread

A good make-ahead. It keeps well.

1 orange, seeded and put through a grinder
1 c. dates
1 c. boiling water and 1 tbsp. added to dates (let cool)

Then add:

> 1 egg, well-beaten
> 1 c. white sugar
> 2 tbsp. milk-free margarine or vegetable shortening
> dash of salt
> 2 c. flour
> 1 tsp. baking powder
> 1 tsp. vanilla
> 4 c. walnut meats

Bake in bread tins at 350° for 50 minutes. Cool before slicing.

CHAPTER 2
CAKES

CAKES HAVE BEEN THE MOST DIFFICULT milk-free or milk-free, egg-free recipes to find, especially those with a light, tasty result. Over twenty years of cooking for a family with milk-free dieters has demanded cupcakes for school parties and cub scout meetings, birthdays and holidays. Some of the following recipes collected and tested should help with these demands.

Superb Feathery Fudge Cake

2/3 c. butter substitute
2 eggs
2½ (1 oz.) squares unsweetened chocolate, melted, cooled
2½ c. cake flour, sifted
½ tsp. salt
1¾ c. sugar
1 tsp. vanilla
1¼ tsp. soda
1¼ c. ice water

Preheat oven to 350°. Blend shortening, sugar, egg and vanilla until fluffy (5 minutes at high speed). Blend in chocolate. Sift flour, soda and salt, then add to combined ingredients, alternating with ice water. Bake in 9-inch round pans 30-35 minutes.

Chocolate Satin Frosting

3½ (1 oz.) squares chocolate
3 c. sifted confectioner's sugar
1 egg
1½ tsp. vanilla
4½ tbsp. hot water
½ c. soft milk-free margarine

Melt chocolate. Blend in sugar and water while warm. Beat in egg, milk-free margarine and vanilla. At this point, place in ice water and beat to proper consistency.

Orange Blossom Cake*

½ c. milk-free margarine
1¾ tsp. vanilla
3 c. sifted cake flour
4 tsp. baking powder
½ c. plus 2 tbsp. milk-substitute
½ c. orange juice
¾ c. granulated sugar
1 tbsp. grated orange rind
1¼ tsp. salt
1¼ tsp. baking soda
yellow food color (optional)

Cream milk-free margarine and sugar until cream colored and light and fluffy. Do not undercream. Beat in vanilla and orange rind. Sift together flour, salt, baking powder and baking soda. Beat together dry ingredients alternately with milk and orange juice. Add yellow color, if desired. Beat batter, at medium speed, for 1 minute. Batter will be of a soft consistency. Divide between two 8-inch layer cake tins, lightly greased and floured. Bake 30 to 35 minutes in 350° oven until cake shrinks from sides. Let cool about one-half hour before turning out of pans. Handle cake carefully, as it is fragile.

FILLING:

1 tbsp. milk-free margarine
1/3 c. sugar
1 c. orange juice
½ tsp. vanilla
⅛ c. cream cornstarch
⅛ tsp. salt
1 egg yolk, slightly beaten

---

*Reprinted with permission from Allergy Information Association, Weston, Ontario, Canada.

Melt milk-free margarine. Blend in cornstarch, sugar and salt. Gradually add orange juice. Heat to boiling over direct heat. Stir into slightly beaten egg yolk. Return to heat and cook 2 minutes, stirring constantly. Add vanilla. Cook slightly then fill the two cake layers with the mixture. Cool thoroughly and then frost. *(Frosting recipe follows)*

ORANGE FROSTING:

> 1 c. granulated sugar
> 1/8 tsp. cream of tartar
> 2 beaten egg whites
> 1 tsp. grated orange rind
> 1 tbsp. white corn syrup
> 1/2 c. water
> 1/4 c. confectioner's sugar
> 1 tbsp. orange juice

Cook sugar, white corn syrup, cream of tartar and water to soft-ball stage, then pour very slowly into egg whites. Beat 10 minutes, then add confectioner's sugar, grated orange rind and orange juice. Beat to spreading consistency.

Chiffon Cake

Angel food and sponge cakes are milk-free and good party cakes. I've only included one—our favorite. It serves sixteen when made in a tube pan and iced or sliced and filled.

> 9-10 lg. eggs, separated (approximately 1 1/4 c. egg whites)
> 1 1/4 c. sugar
> 1 c. cake flour plus 1 tbsp. (sift 2 to 3 times)
> 1/2 tsp. salt
> 1/2 tsp. almond extract
> 1 tsp. water
> 1 tsp. cream of tartar
> 1/2 tsp. vanilla

Beat egg whites in large bowl with salt until frothy, about one minute. Add cream of tartar and beat three minutes, add water and beat on high speed until whites will stand in peaks. Turn mixer to low, add sugar very slowly. Remove from beater and fold in sifted flour very slowly, *do not beat*. Beat egg yolks for a long time until they are pale and thick, add vanilla and almond. Fold into egg whites mixture very slowly, *do not beat*. Bake in angel food tube pan at 325° for 1¼ hours. Test with fingers. If it dents or crackles bake until this does not happen. Cake will often overflow top of the pan. Turn upside down on funnel to cool if this happens, otherwise just turn upside down. (See "Frosting for Chiffon Cake" recipe in "Icing" chapter, this cookbook.)

De Luxe Chiffon Cake

2¼ c. sifted cake flour
1½ c. sugar
3 tsp. baking powder
1 tsp. salt
½ c. vegetable corn oil
6 egg yolks
¾ c. water
1 tsp. grated lemon rind
2 tsp. vanilla
½ tsp. cream of tartar
6 egg whites

Mix and sift first four ingredients. Make a well and add, in order, corn oil, egg yolks, water, lemon rind and vanilla. Beat with spoon until smooth. Add cream of tartar to egg whites. Beat until egg whites form very stiff peaks. Gently fold into first mixture. Pour into ungreased 10-inch tube pan. Bake in slow over (325°F) for 70-75 minutes or until cake springs back when touched lightly with finger. Immediately invert pan over funnel or bottle to cool. Let stand until cold. To remove from pan, loosen side of cake with spatula. May be frosted with any of the frosting you desire. Or bake with 9 x 13-inch pan in moderate oven (350°F) 40 to 45 minutes.

Coffee Rich Pound Cake*

We're proud of this cake—fine, light grain makes a large cake

1½ c. sugar
¾ c. milk-free margarine
1 tbsp. double-action baking powder
1 tsp. salt
1 tsp. vanilla
6 eggs
3¼ c. sifted cake flour
¾ c. Coffee Rich
½ tsp. butter flavoring (if available)

Preheat oven to 350°. Cream together the sugar and milk-free margarine until light and fluffy. Beat in the eggs one at a time. Sift together cake flour, baking powder and salt. Combine Coffee Rich, vanilla and butter flavoring and add alternately with dry ingredients beginning and ending with flour mixture. Pour into three 9-inch wax paper lined or greased and floured cake pans. Bake in 350° oven 25 minutes or until cake pulls away from sides of pan. Remove from pan. Cool. Frost as desired. Yield: Three 9-inch layers. Preparation Time: 40 minutes.

Note: This cake freezes well.
Save one of the layers to use for "Boston Cream Pie."

Milk-Free
Egg-Free

Elaine's Cake—Dark Chocolate

These surprising ingredients turn into a milk-free, egg-free cake, an item very hard to find.

1 c. salad dressing
4 tbsp. cocoa
1 c. warm coffee
¼ tsp. salt
2 c. flour
2 tsp. soda
1 c. white sugar

*Reprinted with permission from Rich Products Corp., 1145 Niagara St. Buffalo, New York.

Mix liquid ingredients. Mix dry ingredients. Then add all ingredients and mix together. Bake at 350° for 35-40 minutes in square pan.

Moist Chocolate Cake

Another rare milk-free, egg-free recipe.

> 2-2/3 c. flour
> 2 tsp. soda
> 2/3 c. cocoa
> 2 c. water
> 2 tsp. vanilla
> 2 c. sugar
> 1 tsp. salt
> 2/3 c. salad oil
> 2 tsp. vinegar

Sift dry ingredients into bowl. Add liquid. Mix well. Bake in 2 greased layer pans or in greased 13 x 9 x 2-inch oblong pan for 30-35 minutes in 350° oven until toothpick comes out clean. Cool and frost.

Note: Batter will be very thin.

Milk-Free
Egg-Free

Fudge Cake

Makes a small layer cake.

> 1¾ c. cake flour
> 2 tsp. baking powder
> ½ tsp. salt
> 1/3 c. shortening
> 1 tsp. vanilla
> 1½ c. sugar
> 4 tbsp. cocoa
> 1½ c. hot water

Sift flour, baking powder and salt together. Blend vanilla and shortening. Add sugar in 6 additions, blending after each addition. Add the cocoa and mix in. Add dry ingredients alternately with water. Beat 20 strokes to insure mixing. Pour batter into pans that are greased on the bottom only. Bake at 350° for 35-40 minutes in two 9-inch layer pans.

Milk-Free
Egg-Free

Scott's Chocolate Cake

A very dark devil's food cake. Beloved favorite of my son who has been on a milk-free diet for twenty years now. Easy, never fails.

1¾ c. all purpose flour, sifted
3 heaping tsp. cocoa
½ tsp. salt
1½ tsp. vinegar
1 c. water
1 tsp. baking soda, rounded
1½ tsp. vanilla
6 tsp. salad oil

Sift dry ingredients together into bowl. Make 3 wells. Pour vanilla in first, salad oil second, and vinegar third. Pour water over all, mix well until smooth. Bake at 350° for 35 minutes in square pan.

Perfect Chocolate Cake

This is an occasion cake, birthday, etc. It takes time to make and frost, but it is worth the effort for the milk-free dieter.

1 c. unsifted unsweetened cocoa
2 c. boiling water
2 tsp. baking soda
½ tsp. baking powder
1 c. milk-free margarine, softened
4 eggs
2¾ c. sifted flour
½ tsp. salt
2½ c. granulated sugar
1½ tsp. vanilla extract

FROSTING:

> 1½ pkg. (6 oz.) semisweet chocolate pieces
> ¾ c. non-dairy frozen creamer
> 1½ c. milk-free margarine
> 3¼ c. sifted confectioner's sugar

FILLING:

> 1 c. non-dairy frozen creamer
> ¼ c. unsifted confectioner's sugar
> 1 tsp. vanilla extract

In medium bowl, combine cocoa with boiling water, mixing with wire whisk until smooth. Cool completely. Sift flour with soda, salt and baking powder. Preheat oven to 350°. Grease well and lightly flour three 9 x 1½-inch layer cake pans. In large bowl of electric mixer, at high speed, beat milk-free margarine, sugar, eggs and vanilla, scraping bowl occasionally, until light—about 5 minutes. At low speed, beat in flour mixture (in fourths), with cocoa mixture (in thirds), beginning and ending with flour mixture. Do not overbeat. Divide evenly into pans, smooth top. Bake 25-30 minutes, or until surface springs back when gently pressed with fingertip. Cool in pans 10 minutes. Carefully loosen sides with spatula, remove from pans, cool on racks.

FROSTING:

In medium saucepan, combine chocolate pieces, non-dairy frozen creamer, and milk-free margarine; stir over medium heat until smooth. Remove from heat. With whisk, blend in 2½ cups confectioner's sugar. In bowl, set over ice and beat until it holds shape.

FILLING:

Whip non-dairy frozen creamer with sugar and vanilla: refrigerate.

TO ASSEMBLE CAKE:

On plate, place a layer, top side down: spread with frosting. Place third layer top side up. Slice top off second layer if it is not flat on both sides.

TO FROST:

With spatula, frost sides first: use rest of frosting on top, swirling decoratively. Refrigerate at least one hour before serving. To cut, use a thin-edged, sharp knife: slice with a sawing motion. Serves 10-12.

Coffee Rich Chocolate Cake*

Preheat oven to 350°

> 1½ c. flour
> ¼ c. cocoa
> ½ tsp. salt
> 1 tsp. vanilla
> 1 c. sugar
> 1 tsp. baking soda
> 1 tbsp. vinegar
> 1-1/3 c. Coffee Rich

Sift all dry ingredients together in mixing bowl. Add remaining ingredients and heat until smooth. Pour batter in greased 9-inch square pan and bake in preheated 350° oven for 30-35 minutes until done. This cake may be decorated with Rich's Richwhip® Topping. Add ¼ cup of confectioner's sugar to 8-ounce carton of Richwhip. (If desired, coloring and flavors may be added at this time.) Whip until stiff peaks are formed. Ice cake as usual.

Maple Cake

If you like maple, you'll like this cake and frosting.

> ½ c. milk-free margarine
> 1 c. maple syrup
> ½ tsp. mace
> 2½ c. flour
> 1 tsp. baking soda
> ½ c. sugar
> 2 eggs
> 1/3 c. water
> 2 tsp. baking powder
> ½ tsp. salt

*Reprinted with permission from Rich Products Corp., 1145 Niagra St., Buffalo, New York.

Cream milk-free margarine with sugar, add syrup and beaten eggs. Beat hard 3 minutes. Add water and dry ingredients sifted together. Heat oven to 350° and bake in loaf pan 30-40 minutes. Frost with maple icing.

Maple Frosting

2 sticks milk-free margarine
1 tbsp. pure vanilla
1/8 tsp. salt
6 c. sifted confectioner's sugar
pinch ground cloves
2/3 c. maple syrup

Combine margarine, vanilla, cloves and salt and beat until fluffy. Add sugar and syrup alternately, blending well. Beat with fork or mixer until it is thick enough to spread.

Pineapple Nut Cake

A milk-free, egg-free recipe, also a delicious treat

1 #2 can crushed pineapple
2½ c. plain flour
½ tsp. salt
1 tsp. soda
1½ c. sugar

Mix above ingredients and bake at 325° for 30-45 minutes.

ICING:

2 sticks milk-free margarine
1 c. cream substitute
1 c. pecans
1 c. Angel Flakes® coconut
1½ c. sugar

Boil 4 minutes. Pour over baked cake while hot in pan. Take a fork and punch holes in cake before pouring icing on.

Marian's Date and Nut Cake

This cake is very quick and easy and is surprisingly good. I usually double it and use a 13 x 9-inch rectangular pan.

1 c. dates
1 c. boiling water
1 c. white sugar
1½ c. flour
1 tsp. soda
½ c. milk-free margarine
1 egg
1 c. nuts

Pour water in with dates and soda. Add margarine while hot. When cool, add sugar, egg, flour and nuts. Bake at 350° for 30-35 minutes in a square pan.

Applesauce Cake

Good rich cake, retains moisture several days.

2½ c. all-purpose flour
1 15-oz. jar applesauce
1/3 c. milk substitute
2 tsp. baking soda
½ tsp. salt
½ tsp. ground cloves
½ c. California walnuts, chopped
1¼ cups sugar
2/3 c. milk-free shortening
2 eggs
1 tsp. cinnamon
½ tsp. nutmeg
1 c. dark seedless raisins

Early in day before serving preheat oven to 350°. Grease and flour a 13 x 9-inch baking pan. Into large bowl, measure all ingredients except raisins and nuts. With mixer at low speed, beat until well-mixed, constantly scraping bowl with rubber spatula. Beat at high speed three minutes, occasionally scraping bowl. Stir in raisins and nuts. Pour batter into pan and bake 40-45 minutes until toothpick inserted in center comes out clean. Cool cake in pan on wire rack. Makes 12 servings.

Milk-Free
Egg-Free

Applesauce Cake

Another easy applesauce cake

1 c. applesauce
2 tsp. warm water
¾ c. flour
2 tsp. soda
¼ tsp. nutmeg
½ c. milk-free margarine
½ tsp. cloves
1 c. brown sugar
½ tsp. cinnamon
1 c. raisins

Mix all ingredients. Bake in a square pan at 375° until cake passes the toothpick test.

Airy Banana Cake

From a newspaper contest

7 lg. eggs, separated
¼ tsp. salt
1 c. finely mashed ripe banana
1 tbsp. frozen orange juice concentrate, undiluted
1 c. sifted cake flour
1 c. sugar
1 tbsp. granted orange rind

In a large mixing bowl beat egg yolks until thickened and lemon colored. Gradually beat in sugar until very thick and ivory colored. Stir in salt, orange rind, banana, concentrate and flour until smooth. In another large mixing bowl, with clean beater, beat egg whites until stiff; fold into banana mixture. Turn into an ungreased 10-inch angel food cake pan. Bake in a preheated 325° oven until cake tester inserted in center comes out clean—about 1 hour. Invert pan on wire rack until cold before removing cake. Cover with orange frosting or glaze. Store in refrigerator. (If cake pan does not have a removable bottom, line bottom with wax paper.)

Milk-Free
Egg-Free

Banana Cake*

¼ c. milk-free shortening
½ tbsp. oil
1½ c. all-purpose flour
¼ c. water
1 tsp. vanilla
1 c. sugar
1 c. mashed bananas
1 tsp. soda
1¼ tsp. baking powder

Blend shortening and sugar. Add oil, water, vanilla and bananas. Sift and stir in dry ingredients. Bake in greased cake pan in 375° oven for 50 minutes.

Spice Cupcakes

Good!

1 c. water
½ c. cold water
1 tbsp. milk-free margarine
1½ tsp. baking powder
½ tsp. allspice
½ tsp. nutmeg
1 c. seeded raisins
1 c. sugar
2 c. bread flour
½ tsp. soda
½ tsp. cinnamon

*Reprinted with permission from Allergy Information Association, Weston, Ontario, Canada.

Boil water and raisins for 10 minutes, then cool. Add cold water to mixture. Separately sift sugar and blend with margarine. Then add the raisin mixture. Sift flour, soda, baking powder, cinnamon, allspice and nutmeg. Add the sifted ingredients in 3 parts to the raisin mixture. Beat after each addition until smooth. Bake in cupcake pans with cupcake papers at 350° for 20 minutes. Frost with brown sugar, carmel or maple frosting.

Pound Cake

1 pound cake flour
1 pound sugar
1 pound eggs (weighed in shells) 9-10 eggs
1 pound milk-free margarine
2 tbsp. vanilla or brandy

Preheat oven to 300°. Sift flour, weigh it and resift. Blend shortening and sugar until fluffy. Add eggs, two at a time and beat well. Add flavoring. Add flour gradually and beat until smooth. Line three bread loaf pans with wax paper. Pour into pans and bake 1 hour and 15 minutes. Slice thin. Serve with tea, coffee or other beverage. May be served with hot lemon sauce, etc.

Milk-Free
Egg-Free

Swedish Tea Cakes

1 c. milk-free margarine
2 egg yolks, slightly beaten
2 c. flour
½ c. dark brown sugar

Blend butter, add sugar and blend again. Add egg yolks and flour and mix well. Roll into balls. Then put balls into egg whites and then into nuts. Bake for 5 minutes in 350° oven and remove. Indent balls with thumb and return to oven for 15 minutes. Remove and fill with preserve.

CHAPTER 3

BAR COOKIES

BAR COOKIES ARE EASIER TO BAKE than drop or rolled cookies. They can be frozen in the pan after baking for later use. They make a complete dessert in themselves.

Milk-Free
Egg-Free

Raisin Mumbles

A very favorite at my house

FILLING:

> ½ c. sugar
> ¼ tsp. salt
> 3 tbsp. lemon juice
> 2½ c. seedless raisins (soak in water)
> 1 c. water
> ½ tsp. cinnamon
> 2 tbsp. cornstarch

Cook over low heat. Stirring until thick and cool.

CRUST:

> ¾ c. soft shortening (milk-free)
> 1 c. brown sugar
> ½ tsp. salt
> 1 c. rolled oats
> 1¾ c. flour
> ½ tsp. soda

Mix shortening and brown sugar. Add flour, salt, soda and rolled oats. Press ½ mixture into greased pan. Spread in filling. Pat on remaining crumbs. Bake at 350° for 20-30 minutes until light brown. Cut into squares.

Raspberry Squares

This is a delicious dessert square.

CAKE:

> 1 c. flour
> 1 tsp. baking powder
> ½ c. milk-free margarine
> 1 egg
> 1 tbsp. milk substitute
> ½ c. raspberry jam

TOPPING:

> 4 tbsp. milk-free margarine
> 1 egg
> 1 c. sugar
> 1 can (4 oz.) coconut
> 1 tsp. vanilla

Preheat oven at 350° and grease an 8-inch square pan. Sift flour and baking powder in a bowl. Cut in milk-free margarine until mixture looks mealy. Beat the egg slightly and stir into flour mixture along with milk substitute. Mix well. Spread dough over bottom of baking pan, cover with a layer of jam. Make up the topping. Melt milk-free margarine. Beat the egg until frothy, then beat in sugar and melted milk-free margarine thoroughly. Chop coconut into smaller pieces, mix with sugar-egg combination. Flavor with vanilla and spread on top of the raspberry jam. Bake 30 minutes. Cool and cut into 16 squares.

Cherry-Walnut Bars

Very good—Pretty for parties

> 2¼ c. sifted flour
> 1 c. milk-free margarine
> 1½ c. brown sugar, firmly packed
> ½ tsp. salt
> ½ c. chopped maraschino cherries, drained
> ½ c. sugar
> 2 whole eggs
> 1 egg yolk
> ½ tsp. baking powder
> 1 c. chopped English walnuts

Sift two cups of the flour and white sugar, cut in milk-free margarine. Pat into greased 9 x 13-inch baking pan. Bake in moderate oven (350°) for 12 minutes. Beat eggs, egg yolk and brown sugar until fluffy. Stir remaining ¼ cup flour with baking powder and salt. Blend into egg mixture. Stir in cherries and nuts. Spread mixture over baked crust; bake 20-25 minutes longer and cool in pan on rack. Frost with cherry icing if desired. Yields about 4 dozen bars.

CHERRY ICING:

Combine one lightly beaten egg white, two tablespoons maraschino cherry juice and about two cups powdered sugar. Beat until smooth.

Milk-Free
Egg-Free

Raspberry Squares II*

1¼ c. sifted flour
1¼ c. quick rolled oats
⅞ c. melted milk-free margarine
¾ c. raspberry jam
1 c. brown sugar
pinch of salt

Mix all ingredients except jam together. Press half of mixture into greased 8 x 8-inch pan. Cover with jam. Spread rest of mixture over jam. Bake at 350° for 30 minutes. Cut into squares.

---

*Reprinted with permission from Allergy Information Association, Weston, Ontario, Canada.

Milk-Free
Egg-Free

Cherry Squares II*

¾ c. milk-free margarine
1½ c. flour
2 envelopes gelatin
1 tsp. almond flavoring
½ c. chopped cherries
1/3 c. brown sugar
½ c. cold water
2 c. white sugar
½ c. warm water
½ c. chopped almonds (optional)

Cream margarine and sugar. Add flour and mix well. Put in greased 9 x 12-inch pan and bake at 350° for about 25 minutes. Cool. Dissolve gelatin in cold water. Set aside. Boil white sugar and warm water for two minutes. Combine with gelatin mixture and beat until stiff. Add rest of ingredients and pour on top of baked mixture. Let set and cut into squares.

Lemon Squares

Use for a party with Raspberry Squares and Cherry Walnut Bars.

½ c. milk-free margarine
1 c. firmly packed light brown sugar
½ tsp. vanilla
½ c. chopped walnuts
1 tbsp. flour
¾ c. flaked coconut
1 c. sifted flour
½ tsp. baking powder
1 large egg
¼ tsp. salt
Lemon Glaze (see below)

---

*Reprinted with permission from Allergy Information Association, Weston, Ontario, Canada.

In a medium mixing bowl blend the milk-free margarine and ½ cup of the sugar; gradually stir in the cup of flour. Firmly pat the mixture over the bottom of a rectangular greased baking pan. Bake in a preheated 325° oven about 20 minutes—do not brown. In a small mixing bowl beat egg until it is thickened and lemon colored: gradually beat in the remaining ½ cup sugar and the vanilla. Stir together the 1 tablespoon flour, baking powder and salt; beat into egg mixture; and fold in walnuts and coconut. As soon as bottom layer is baked, spread this mixture over it. Return to 325° oven until toast colored—about 25 minutes. Cool. With a small metal spatula loosen edges, turn out on cutting board, turn right side up, cover top with Lemon Glaze and let set. With a sharp, heavy knife, cut into small squares. Stores well in a tightly covered tin box for a day or two.

LEMON GLAZE:

> 1 tbsp. milk-free margarine
> ¼ tsp. grated lemon rind
> 1¼ c. confectioner's sugar
> 2 tbsp. lemon juice

Beat together margarine, confectioner's sugar, lemon rind and lemon juice.

Choco-Nut Dream Bars

Worth the effort

> 2/3 c. sugar
> ½ tsp. vanilla
> ¼ tsp. salt
> ½ c. soft milk-free margarine
> 1 c. sifted all-purpose flour

Combine all ingredients except the flour; beat until blended. Gradually stir in flour. Press over bottom of ungreased 13 x 9 x 2-inch pan. Bake in 350 degree oven, 16-18 minutes. Cool 5 minutes. Cover with topping.

TOPPING:

> 1 c. sugar
> 1 tsp. vanilla
> 3 c. finely chopped nuts
> 2 eggs
> ¾ tsp. salt

Combine all ingredients except the nuts, beat until light. Blend in nuts. Spread over cooled baked layer. Bake in 350° oven for 20 minutes. Cool. Frost with Chocolate Frosting.

CHOCOLATE FROSTING:

> ½ c. non-dairy frozen creamer
> 1 6-oz. package semisweet chocolate pieces
> dash of salt
> 1 tsp. vanilla

Combine milk substitute (non-dairy frozen creamer) and salt in saucepan; bring just to a boil over moderate heat. Add semisweet chocolate morsels and vanilla; stir until smooth. Cool until thick enough to spread. Spread over top of baked mixture. Cool. Cut into 2 x 1-inch bars. Garnish with slivered almonds or chopped nuts. Yields 48 bars.

Mother's Brownies

Superb

> 2 eggs
> 1 c. sugar
> ½ c. flour
> ½ c. vegetable shortening melted with 2 squares semi-sweet chocolate
> ½ c. chopped nuts
> 1 tsp. vanilla
> ¼ tsp. salt
> ¼ tsp. baking powder

Mix. Spread in flat pan. Bake at 350°, 30-40 minutes. (Note: This recipe is fairly small, but larger amounts can easily be made by proportionately increasing the ingredients.)

Blond Brownies

Good Change

> ¼ c. soft shortening
> 1½ c. brown sugar
> 1½ tsp. baking powder
> ½ c. semisweet chocolate pieces
> 2 eggs
> 1 c. flour
> ½ tsp. salt
> ½ c. chopped nuts

Mix ingredients together. Bake in greased square cake pan for 30 minutes in a 350° oven.

CHAPTER 4

COOKIES

THESE DELIGHTFUL SNACKS are the great treats of childhood. Most adults, too, enjoy a freshly baked cookie as a breakfast bit, a lunch supplement, a coffee or tea treat, a snack, or even for a dinner dessert.

Helping to make and bake cookies always intrigues children, and the anticipation of the sweet is half the fun.

My recipe collection grew because my children always volunteered my services as a cookie provider at school or scout or church events.

I hope you enjoy them as much as we do.

Milk-Free
Egg-Free

Unbaked Chocolate Oatmeal Cookies*

A combination cookie and candy, fun for the younger set to make

1 stick (½ c.) milk-free margarine
2 c. granulated sugar
½ c. Coffee Rich
3 c. quick-cooking oatmeal
1 c. shredded coconut
¼ c. cocoa
1 c. raisins

In heavy sauce pan, mix together butter, sugar, cocoa and Coffee Rich. Bring to a boil and, with stirring, boil for 2 minutes. Remove from heat. Stir oatmeal, coconut and raisins into sugar-Coffee Rich mixture. Drop by teaspoonfuls onto wax paper. Cool.

*Reprinted with permission from Rich Products Corp., P.O. Box 245, 1145 Niagara Street, Buffalo, New York 14240.

Yield: 4 dozen cookies.
Preparation time: 15 minutes.

Snickerdoodles

Very nice white cookie

½ c. milk-free margarine
2 eggs
¼ tsp. salt
2 tsp. cinnamon
2¾ c. flour
½ c. shortening
2 tsp. cream of tartar
1½ c. sugar
1 tsp. soda
2 tbsp. sugar

Heat oven to 400°. Thoroughly mix milk-free margarine, shortening, 1½ cups sugar, and eggs. Blend in flour, cream of tartar, soda and salt. Shape dough into balls. Mix 2 tablespoons of sugar and the cinnamon, roll balls in mixture. Place 2 inches apart on ungreased sheet. Bake 8-10 minutes or until set. Immediately remove from baking sheet. Frost if desired. Yields 6 dozen.

Milk-Free
Egg-Free

Shortbread Cookies*

½ lb. milk-free margarine
2 c. flour
2 tsp. cornstarch (level)
½ c. powdered sugar
salt

---

*Reprinted with permission from Allergy Information Association, Weston, Ontario, Canada.

Cream milk-free margarine and sugar. Add dry ingredients and mix thoroughly. Roll a small amount of dough in hand to form a ball, press center with thumb and decorate with a little jam or sprinkle with colored sugar. Place on ungreased pan and bake in a 350° oven until slightly brown.

Milk-Free
Egg-Free

Raisin Cookies†

1 c. brown sugar
1 c. raisins
2 tbsp. shortening
¾ tsp. soda
1 tsp. cinnamon
1 c. water
½ tsp. salt
1½ c. flour
½ tsp. ginger

Cook together sugar, water, raisins, fat and salt. Let cool. Sift dry ingredients together and stir into cooled mixture. Drop by teaspoonfuls on to baking sheet and bake in 350° oven for 15 minutes.

Milk-Free
Egg-Free

Bonbon Cookies

Can be beautiful and delicious. Use different colored pastel tinted icing and suggested topping. Not difficult.

½ c. milk-free margarine
¾ c. sifted confectioner's sugar
food coloring if desired
⅛ tsp. salt
1 tbsp. vanilla
1½ c. flour

---

†Reprinted with permission from Allergy Information Association, Weston, Ontario, Canada.

FILLINGS: candied or maraschino cherries, pitted dates, nuts or chocolate pieces, bonbon icing.

TOPPINGS: chopped nuts, coconut, colored sugar, glazed cherries.

Mix milk-free margarine, sugar, vanilla and food coloring. Blend in flour and salt thoroughly by hand. If dough is dry add 1 to 2 table-spoons non-dairy frozen creamer (see introduction). Heat oven to 350°. For each cookie, wrap one level tablespoon of dough around a filling suggested above. Bake one inch apart on ungreased baking sheet 12 to 15 minutes or until set, but not brown. Cool; dip tops of cookies in milk-free white or colored icings, and decorate with toppings suggested. Makes 20 to 25 cookies. *(Note: Do not use self-rising flour in this recipe)*

Soft Sugar Cookies

It is hard to get a milk-free sugar cookie
Mix in order given:

> 1 c. white sugar
> 1 c. non-dairy frozen creamer + 1 tsp. lemon juice
> 1 c. shortening
> 1 tsp. lemon flavoring
> ½ c. brown sugar
> 2 eggs

Sift 3½ cups all-purpose flour, 1 teaspoon baking powder and 1 tea-spoon salt. Add alternately with following: 1 teaspoon soda with 1 cup non-dairy frozen creamer and 1 teaspoon lemon juice. Drop by heaping teaspoons on greased tin. Flatten with fork dipped in milk. Sprinkle with sugar and bake at 350° until light brown. Do not overbake.

Soft White Cookies

As above—only this is a rolled cookie. Good for child to cut and decorate for holidays or parties.

1 c. white sugar
1½ c. milk-free margarine
vanilla or lemon flavoring
½ tsp. ginger or nutmeg (optional)
2 lg. eggs
3 tbsp. cold water
1 tsp. soda

Use enough flour to roll out, have dough as soft as can be rolled and handled. Cut and bake in 350° oven until golden brown.

Chocolate Date-Nut Chews

Try these for a real treat

½ tsp. salt
¾ c. flour
½ c. granulated sugar
½ c. grated semisweet chocolate
1 c. chopped dates
¼ tsp. baking powder
1 c. brown sugar
1 c. chopped nuts
2 eggs, well-beaten

Sift salt, baking powder and flour together. Add brown sugar, granulated sugar, chocolate, dates and nuts. Whip in well-beaten eggs. Pour mixture in well-greased 8 x 8-inch pan. Bake in 375° oven for 30-40 minutes. Cool and spread chocolate fudge icing on top.

Chocolate Fudge Icing

2 c. sugar
3 oz. semisweet chocolate
1 tsp. vanilla
2 tbsp. corn syrup
½ c. non-dairy frozen creamer
2 tbsp. Crisco®

Cook sugar, syrup, chocolate and non-dairy frozen creamer until mixture forms a soft ball when dropped into cold water. Remove from heat. Add vanilla and milk-free margarine. Let cool and beat until thick enough to spread.

Almond Cookies

Double the recipe, they will disappear quickly

> 2 c. all-purpose flour
> ½ c. packed light brown sugar
> ½ c. milk-free shortening, softened
> 1 tsp. double acting baking powder
> ¼ tsp. baking soda
> 2 eggs
> ½ tsp. ground cardamon (optional)
> ¾ tsp. almond extract
> 20 whole almonds
> ½ c. sugar
> ½ tsp. salt

Preheat oven to 350°. Into large bowl measure all ingredients except almonds. Mix at low speed. Beat ingredients until mixed. Increase to medium and beat 2 minutes, scraping bowl sides occasionally. On lightly floured surface divide into 20 equal pieces. With hands, roll dough into balls and place about 2 inches apart on ungreased cookie sheet. Flatten with bottom of glass. Put almond in center. Bake 12-15 minutes until lightly browned around the edges. Remove immediately to wire rack. Store in tightly covered container up to 2 weeks. Makes 20 cookies.

Almond Flower Cakes

Tiny cakes

> ¾ c. sugar
> 2 c. unsifted all-purpose flour
> 1 c. milk-free margarine
> raspberry or currant jelly
> 1 tsp. almond extract
> 2 egg yolks, beaten

Sift flour and sugar into a large bowl. Cut each stick of milk-free margarine into 8 pieces; with pastry blender or 2 knives, cut milk-free margine into flour mixture until it resembles coarse cornmeal. Combine almond extract and egg yolks; pour into flour mixture, mixing with hands just until smooth. Divide dough in half. Preheat oven to 375°. Lightly grease two ¾-inch cupcake pans. Between two sheets of waxed paper, roll out dough, one part at a time, ½ inch thick. Cut with a floured 2½-inch scalloped cookie cutter. Repeat with other half of dough. Fit into prepared cupcake pans. With finger, make an imprint in center of each: fill each with jam. Bake 15 minutes or until golden-brown. Let cool in pans a few minutes; turn out on wire rack to cool completely. Fill indentations with more jam, if necessary. Makes 24.

Almond Sticks

Good holiday cookie

>   ¾ c. milk-free margarine
>   2 c. flour, sifted
>   1 tsp. almond flavoring
>   1 egg white, slightly beaten
>   ¼ c. sugar
>   1 tbsp. sugar
>   1/3 c. chopped almonds

Mix milk-free margarine with ¼ cup sugar and almond flavoring together thoroughly. Stir in sifted flour. Mix with hands. Chill. Roll out ¼-inch thick. Cut into strips 2½ inches wide. Brush tops with egg white. Sprinkle with mixture of sugar and finely chopped blanched almonds. Bake at 350° for about 17 minutes on ungreased cookie sheet or until just golden.

Ginger Soft Cookies

Good breakfast cookie or any time of day

>   ¾ c. milk-free margarine
>   1 egg
>   1 c. sugar
>   ¼ c. molasses

Mix together thoroughly.
Sift and stir in:

> 2 c. flour
> ¼ tsp. salt
> ½ tsp. cloves
> 2 tsp. soda
> 1 tsp. cinnamon
> ¾ tsp. ginger

Form into balls the size of small walnuts. Place 2 inches apart on ungreased cookie sheet and bake 10-20 minutes in a 375° oven. Roll in confectioner's sugar while warm.

Ginger Crisps

Similar to ginger snaps

> 2 c. all-purpose flour
> ¾ c. Crisco
> ½ c. dark molasses
> 1½ tsp. cinnamon
> ½ tsp. nutmeg
> 1 c. sugar
> 1 egg
> 1½ tsp. ginger
> 1 tsp. salt

In a large bowl mix flour, sugar and remaining ingredients. Use mixer at low speed, beat together ingredients until just mixed; increase speed to medium and beat 2 minutes, occasionally scraping bowl with rubber spatula. Wrap in wax paper; refrigerate 1 hour or until slightly firm so it is easy to handle. Preheat oven to 375°. On lightly floured surface divide into teaspoon-sized pieces. With hands, roll into balls, coat with sugar. Place 2 inches apart on greased cookie sheet. Flatten with bottom of flat glass to $\frac{1}{8}$ inch thick. Bake 8-10 minutes until edges are lightly brown. Cool 2 minutes on sheet. Then remove to wire racks to cool.

Milk-Free
Egg-Free

Old Fashioned Lace Cookies

1 c. flour
dash nutmeg
½ tsp. soda
¾ tsp. baking powder
½ c. milk-free margarine
1 tsp. cinnamon
¼ tsp. salt
½ c. sugar
½ c. molasses
1 tsp. lemon extract

Mix. Bake at 325° for 12-15 minutes.

Gingerbread Men

Up to a week before serving:

Sift together 1¾ cups sifted rye flour*, ½ teaspoon salt, ½ teaspoon double-acting baking powder, ½ teaspoon baking soda, 1 teaspoon ginger and 1 teaspoon cinnamon. In a medium bowl, with an electric mixer at medium speed, cream ¼ cup hydrogenated shortening with ½ cup granulated sugar until light and fluffy. Add 1 egg: beat thoroughly. Slowly beat in ¼ cup molasses. Stir in dry ingredients until just mixed. Using the electric mixer, beat until smooth and extremely sticky. Cover: refrigerate at least 6 hours and preferably overnight.

When ready to bake cookies:

Start heating oven to 350°F. Grease cookie sheets. Generously flour pastry cloth or board and rolling pin with rye flour. Roll dough ⅛ to 3/16 of an inch thick. Using gingerbread man cookie cutter, cut cookies. With wide spatula, transfer to cookie sheets. Bake 12 to 14 minutes, or until cookies begin to brown lightly. Re-

---

*If rye flour is coarsely milled, sift it with a very fine sieve and use only the finest particles.

move immediately. Cool on flat surface. Chill dough scraps at least 15 minutes before rerolling as directed above.

To decorate the cookies:

Prepare Ornamental Frosting as follows: Sift 1½ cups sifted confectioner's sugar with ⅛ teaspoon cream of tartar. In a medium bowl, stir together this mixture, ¼ teaspoon vanilla extract, and 1 egg white. With electric mixer at highest speed, beat until frosting is so thick that a knife drawn through it leaves a clean-cut path. (This will take at least 5 minutes.) If necessary, add more sugar to make mixture desired consistency. If you wish, add food color to all or part of the frosting. Using this frosting and pastry bag, decorate cookies. Add colored granulated sugar, dragees, chocolate morsels, etc. for finishing touches. When frosting has hardened, store cookies in an air-tight container. Makes about sixteen 5-inch cookies.

Applesauce Molasses Cookies

These keep well and can be made a few each day, if desired, from refrigerated dough.

3 c. sifted cake flour
1½ tsp. baking soda
1½ tsp. cinnamon
1 c. sugar
½ c. light molasses
1 c. canned applesauce
½ tsp. salt
1 tsp. ginger
½ c. milk-free shortening
1 egg, unbeaten
½ tsp. vanilla

Sift flour with soda, salt and spices. Blend shortening: add sugar gradually, beating until light. Add egg and beat well, then stir in molasses. Add flour alternately with applesauce, mixing well after each addition. Stir in vanilla. Chill until firm enough to hold shape—1 to 2 hours. Drop from teaspoon on lightly greased baking sheets, placing about 2 inches apart. If desired, add a garnish to cookies before baking (nut halves or a sprinkling of colored sugar). Bake at 400° for 8-10 minutes or until done. Cool on wire rack. Makes 6 dozen. (Note: Chill cookie dough between baking, if necessary.)

Milk-Free
Egg-Free

Unbaked Cookies

Keep well

> 2 c. graham cracker crumbs
> ¼ tsp. nutmeg
> 1 c. nuts
> 4 tbsp. milk-free margarine
> ¼ tsp. salt
> 1 c. dates
> 1¼ tbsp. fruit juice
> Rye, bourbon or rum

Mix by hand. No baking.

Milk-Free
Egg-Free

Molasses Cookies

An egg-free rolled molasses cookie

> 2 c. molasses
> ½ c. milk-free margarine
> ½ tsp. ginger
> 3 tsp. soda in 1 c. of boiling water
> ½ c. sugar
> 1 c. melted lard
> 1 qt. to 3 pts. flour

Mix. Let stand until cool. Roll out. Cut and bake.

Soft Molasses Cookies

This is from an old family recipe and is a soft, delicious cookie.

1 c. molasses
1 tsp. cream of tartar
1 c. sugar
1 egg (or 1 tbsp. orange juice and 1 tsp. vegetable oil)
1½ c. part milk-free margarine and part lard
2 heaping tsp. soda
4 c. flour or more
1 c. warm water
1 tsp. ginger
1 tsp. salt

(Make a test cookie to see if flour is sufficient.) Chill and drop from spoon to bake. May be made in parts, and dough will keep over a week or so in refrigerator if covered.

Oatmeal Cookies #I

Good child's cookies

½ c. shortening
1 egg
½ tsp. baking soda
1 c. old fashioned or quick-cooking oats, uncooked
¾ c. all purpose flour
½ c. packed light brown sugar
½ c. chopped California walnuts or raisins (optional)
¼ c. sugar
½ tsp. salt
½ tsp. vanilla extract

Early in day or up to 2 weeks before serving: preheat oven to 375°. Into large bowl, measure all ingredients. With mixer at low speed, beat ingredients until just mixed: increase speed to medium and beat 4 minutes, occasionally scraping bowl with rubber spatula.

Drop by teaspoonfuls, 1 inch apart, onto ungreased cookie sheets. Bake 10-12 minutes or until lightly browned. With pancake turner, immediately remove cookies to wire racks: cool. Store in tightly covered container. Makes about 3 dozen.

Crisp Oatmeal Cookies #II

More crisp than oatmeal cookie #I

> 2 c. shortening
> 4 eggs
> 1 tsp. salt
> 5½ c. quick-cooking oatmeal
> 2½ c. brown sugar, firmly packed
> 5 tsp. soda, dissolved in ½ c. water
> 2 c. sugar
> 5½ c. flour
> 2 tsp. vanilla
> 3 c. (15 oz.) raisins (optional)

In large mixer bowl, blend sugars with the shortening. Add eggs, one at a time, while beating. Add water mixed with soda, the salt, and vanilla. Still in the mixer, blend in about half the flour, stopping when the mixer begins to feel overworked. Transfer mixture to a huge bowl and mix in the rest of the flour and oatmeal. The best possible tool for stirring up such a quantity is the human hand. If you use raisins, work them in last. Form into 5 or 6 rolls, 1½ to 2 inches in diameter, depending upon how large you like them. Freezing for a couple of hours makes them easy to slice for baking. Slice 5 or 6 cookies to the inch and bake at 375° for 10-12 minutes on ungreased baking sheets. These cookies will keep indefinitely in the freezer. Makes 12-15 dozen.

Milk-Free
Egg-Free

Oatmeal Date Balls #III

A different oatmeal cookie—good

1 c. milk-free margarine
3 tbsp. sugar
1½ tsp. cinnamon
2 8-oz. packages whole pitted dates, finely chopped
1 c. quick-cooking or old-fashioned oats
¾ c. finely chopped nuts (optional)

Early in day: in large bowl with mixer at medium speed, beat first three ingredients until fluffy. With spoon, stir in dates and oats. Cover and refrigerate dough 2-3 hours until firm. With hands, shape dough into 1-inch balls; roll in nuts. Chill. Makes about 3½ dozen.

Milk-Free
Egg-Free

Brandy Snaps

Adult cookies—delicious party treats

¼ c. light corn syrup
½ c. milk-free margarine
2/3 c. sugar
2 tsp. brandy
¼ c. molasses
1 c. sifted flour
1 tsp. ground ginger

Preheat oven to 300°. Heat the syrup and molasses to boiling. Remove from heat and add milk-free margarine. Sift together flour, sugar and ginger. Add gradually, while stirring, to molasses mixture. Mix well. Add brandy. Drop by half-teaspoonfuls three inches apart on a greased cookie sheet. Bake 10 minutes. Remove from oven, loosen one cookie at a time, and roll over handle of a wooden spoon. Slip off carefully. Serve filled with non-dairy whipped topping. Yield: 18 cookies.

Milk-Free
Egg-Free

Nut Crunch Cookies

Very good for young children

>   2 tsp. vegetable oil
>   1 c. milk-free margarine
>   1 c. well-chopped nuts
>   15-18 graham crackers (milk free)
>   1 c. brown sugar

Pour oil into a 10 x 15-inch jelly roll pan, tilting in all directions. Break crackers into quarters, arranging on bottom of pan as close together as possible. Melt shortening, add sugar and bring to a boil, stirring. Boil exactly 2 minutes. Pour over graham crackers. Sprinkle with nuts. Bake at 350° for 10 minutes. Cool in pan. Break when cool.

Milk-Free
Egg-Free

Melt-Aways

An elegant cookie, but do not make too far ahead: it does not keep well.

>   1 c. milk-free margarine
>   1¼ c. confectioner's sugar
>   1¼ c. sifted flour
>   9 oz .bar semisweet chocolate, melted
>   1 tsp. vanilla
>   ½ tsp. salt
>   1 c. walnuts, grated

Blend milk-free margarine, adding sugar gradually. Add vanilla. Resift flour with salt. Add, with grated walnuts, to mixture. Melt chocolate over hot water and blend into above mixture. Shape into balls, using one teaspoon of dough for each and place on greased cookie sheets. (These will spread during baking.) Bake in moderately low (250°) oven about 40 minutes. Yield: 11 dozen.

Pecan Rounds

Try these for a treat or tea party

1 c. milk-free margarine
1½ c. chopped pecans
4 rounded tsp. sugar
2 tsp. vanilla
2 c. cake flour

Bake at 300°, 40-45 minutes. Roll in powdered sugar while warm and again when cool.

CHAPTER 5
CONFECTIONS & FROZEN DESSERTS
ICING-FROSTINGS

M ost icing recipes are easily made by using vegetable shortening in place of butter and non-dairy frozen creamer to replace milk or cream in the recipe.

> Boiled Frosting
> 7-Minute Frosting
> "Butter" Frosting
> Chocolate Frosting
> Maple or Caramel Frosting

These can all be made by substituting the above.

Milk-Free
Egg-Free

Marshmallow Basic*

1/3 c. water
½ c. sugar
2/3 c. sugar cane syrup
1 tsp. vanilla
1 env. unflavored gelatin

Mix water, gelatin and sugar together in a saucepan. Heat until sugar and gelatin are dissolved. Pour sugar cane syrup into a large bowl: add hot mixture and vanilla. Beat on high speed of mixer for 15 minutes, until mixture is thick

Use as a garnish for jellies and other desserts in place of whipped cream, or as a filling and frosting for cakes.

---

*Reprinted with permission from Allergy Information Association, Weston, Ontario, Canada.

Frosting for Chiffon Cake

2 c. sugar
3 egg whites
1 tsp. vanilla
1 c. water
1 tsp. cream of tartar

Boil sugar and water until it threads from the spoon. Pour slowly into the egg whites previously beaten until stiff with the cream of tartar. Pour in a slow stream, keeping beater at high speed. (Sometimes I do not use all of the syrup.) Add the vanilla. Frost quickly and generously. Add decorations before it sets.

For other frostings in Cakes and Desserts chapters, see icings index listing.

Recipes for Refrigerator Ice Cream*

Lemon-Strawberry Ice Cream

2 eggs
2 c. (1 pt.) Coffee Rich
½ c. light corn syrup
½ c. sugar
¼ c. lemon juice
1 c. crushed and sweetened strawberries

Beat eggs slightly. Gradually add sugar and beat until light and lemon colored. Beat in Coffee Rich, lemon juice and corn syrup. Pour into 2 refrigerator trays and freeze until firm. Break ice cream into chunks. Turn into bowl and beat until light and fluffy. Fold in crushed strawberries. Return to freezer trays: freeze until firm. Yield: 8-10 servings.

---

*Reprinted with permission from Rich Products Corp., P.O. Box 245, 1145 Niagara St., Buffalo, New York.

Easy Refrigerator Sherbet*

1 3-oz. pkg. flavored gelatin†
1 c. hot water
¼ c. lemon juice
3 c. Coffee Rich
½ c. sugar

Dissolve gelatin in hot water. Add Coffee Rich, lemon juice and sugar to gelatin, blending well. Pour into 2 refrigerator trays and freeze until firm. Break sherbet into chunks: turn into bowl. With electric beater whip until smooth. Return to cold trays. Freeze until firm. Yield: 8-10 servings.

Perfect Fruit Sherbet

1 tbsp. unflavored gelatin
¼ c. cold water
1 c. minus 2 tbsp. sugar
1 c. sweetened crushed fruit‡
2 tbsp. sugar
2 c. (1 pt.) Coffee Rich
1 egg white

Soften gelatin in cold water; dissolve over hot water. Blend Coffee Rich, sugar and crushed fruit until sugar is dissolved. Beat in dissolved gelatin mixture. Pour into 2 refrigerator trays and freeze until firm. Break sherbet into chunks, turn into bowl. With electric beater whip until smooth. Beat egg white until foamy, gradually add 2 tbsp. sugar and beat until stiff. Fold into sherbet mixture. Return to refrigerator trays and freeze until firm. Yield: 8-10 servings.

---

*Reprinted with permission from Rich Products Corp., P.O. Box 245, 1145 Niagara St., Buffalo, N.Y.

†Lemon, lime, raspberry, etc.

‡Pineapple, strawberries, red raspberries, fruit cocktail, etc.

Recipes for Mechanical Ice Cream Freezer

Milk-Free
Egg-Free

Pineapple Sherbet

1 qt. Coffee Rich
2 c. crushed pineapple
crushed ice
1½ c. sugar
½ c. light corn syrup
ice cream salt

Mix together all ingredients until sugar is dissolved. Freeze until firm using 8 parts ice to 1 part salt. Yield: 2½ quarts.

Milk-Free
Egg-Free

Orange Velvet Sherbet

1 qt. Coffee Rich
3½ c. orange juice (1 6-oz. can frozen, reconstituted orange juice)
1 tbsp. unflavored gelatin
¼ c. cold water
½ c. lemon juice
3 c. sugar
ice cream salt
crushed ice

Blend together Coffee Rich, citrus juices and sugar until sugar is dissolved. Dissolve gelatin in cold water. Melt over water bath. With beating, add to Coffee Rich mixture until well blended. Freeze until firm using 8 parts ice to 1 part salt. Yield: 2½ quarts.

*Reprinted with permission from Rich Products Corp., P.O. Box 245, 1145 Niagara St., Buffalo, N.Y.

Milk-Free
Egg-Free

Chocolate Ice Cream (Cocoa)

> 1 c. sugar
> 1 qt. Coffee Rich
> ½ c. cocoa
> 1/3 c. corn syrup
> ice cream salt
> crushed ice

Blend together sugar and cocoa. Blend together Coffee Rich and corn syrup; add gradually to cocoa sugar. Mix all until well-blended. Freeze until firm using 8 parts ice to 1 part salt.

Milk-Free
Egg-Free

Philadelphia or Plain Ice Cream

BASIC RECIPE:

> 1 qt. Coffee Rich
> 1 tsp. vanilla
> ¾ c. sugar
> 1 pinch salt
> crushed ice
> ice cream salt
> (I use sidewalk salt from winter pack-up)

Mix all ingredients to dissolve sugar. Freeze until firm using 8 parts ice to 1 part salt. Yield: 1½ quarts.

COFFEE: Dissolve 1-1½ tablespoons instant coffee in 2 tablespoons hot water and add to ice cream mixture.

MAPLE NUT: Add 1 cup finely chopped nuts and substitute maple flavoring for vanilla in ice cream mix.

PEPPERMINT STICK: Substitute ½ pound crushed peppermint stick candy for sugar and vanilla. Tint a delicate pink color if desired.

Fruit Ice*

1 14-oz. can apricots, plums or peaches
1 c. water
2 egg whites, stiffly beaten
¾ c. corn syrup
1/3 c. lemon juice

Empty fruit and syrup into strainer placed over a bowl: press fruit through strainer (or blend in blender). Reserve. Combine water, corn syrup and sugar in saucepan. Bring to boil, stirring until sugar dissolves and boil 5 minutes. Cool. Add lemon juice and fruit purée. Turn into freezing tray or trays and freeze until ice crystals form. Turn almost-frozen mixture into bowl and beat until smooth. Fold in beaten egg whites. Return to tray and continue freezing until firm. Yield: about 1 quart.

Fruit Ice†

1 container any strained baby fruit
1 tbsp. corn syrup
1 egg white, beaten stiff
2 tbsp. lemon juice

Combine ingredients and freeze until firm. Remove to a chilled bowl, beat until free of hard lumps but still thick. Place in chilled sherbet or sauce dish (or paper souffle cups) and finish freezing.

---

*Reprinted with permission from Allergy Information Association, Weston, Ontario, Canada.

†Reprinted with permission from Allergy Information Association, Weston, Ontario, Canada.

Banana Pineapple Sherbet*

1½ c. crushed pineapple
¾ c. confectioner's sugar
1½ c. banana pulp (about 3 large bananas)
½ c. orange juice
6 tbsp. lemon juice
2 egg whites

Combine pineapple and sugar. Stir until dissolved. Add banana and juices. Place in refrigerator trays and freeze until nearly firm. Beat egg whites until stiff but not dry. Add fruit mixture gradually. Beat sherbet until light and fluffy. Return to trays and freeze until firm.

Milk-Free
Egg-Free

Imitation Ice Cream Bars and Fudgesicles†

Whip lightly frozen Richwhip, place in Tupperware® Ice Tubs, insert wooden popsicles stick and freeze. (It will not freeze hard enough to stick to the popsicle sticks when too fluffy.)

FUDGSICLES: Make a syrup of ½ cup sugar, ½ cup water and 12 ounces package Baker's Semi-Sweet Chocolate Chips melted down in top of a double boiler. Cool. Add ½ cup of this mixture to one package of Richwhip. Place in Tupperware Ice Tubs, insert wooden popsicle stick, and freeze. Bars and fudgsicles can be removed from Ice Tubs and stored in freezer. (Wooden popsicles sticks can be purchased through stationery or hobby shops.)

---

*Reprinted with permission from Allergy Information Association, Weston, Ontario, Canada.
†Reprinted with permission from Allergy Information Association, Weston, Ontario, Canada.

Milk-Free
Egg-Free

"Isomil" Imitation Ice Cream*

Refrigerator Tray Method:

1-13-oz. can Isomil® concentrate, well-chilled (do not dilute with water)
1½ teaspoons unflavored gelatin: soften in 2 tbsp. cold water
¼ c. sugar—add to the gelatin and heat slowly to dissolve sugar and gelatin: cool.
2 tbsp. clear corn syrup
1 tbsp. salad or cooking oil
2 tbsp. vanilla extract

Blend all ingredients in a blender until thick and creamy. Pour into an ice cube tray or a loaf pan and freeze until very icy. Turn into blender and blend until smooth. Return to freezer and freeze until firm. Allow to soften slightly before serving. Blender capacity for this recipe should be at least 5 cups.

Milk-Free
Egg-Free

Creamy Coffee Frosting*

At least 20 minutes before frosting cake:

In a medium bowl, with electric mixer at low speed, thoroughly blend ⅔ cup hydrogenated shortening with 4 cups sifted confectioner's sugar. Beat in 6 tablespoons boiling water, 1 tablespoon instant-coffee powder, 2 teaspoons vanilla extract and ¼ teaspoon salt. With mixer at low speed, beat in enough sifted confectioner's sugar (about 2 cups) to make a frosting with a good spreading consistency. Beat, at high speed, 1 minute. Use to frost about 36

---

*Reprinted with permission from Allergy Information Association, Weston, Ontario, Canada.

†Individual flavor variations: Fruits such as strawberries, peaches, bananas, pineapple, oranges, etc. may be added to the recipe prior to freezing after being mashed or pureed in a blender, depending upon individual tastes and allergies.

cupcakes or one 13 × 9 × 2-inch oblong cake to fill and frost an 8 × 9-inch layer cake.

Milk-Free
Egg-Free

Creamy Chocolate Frosting

Mix 6 tablespoons cocoa with shortening and sugar: omit instant coffee: prepare as directed, above.

Milk-Free
Egg-Free

Creamy Apricot Frosting

Heat one 4¾-ounce jar strained apricots with tapioca almost to a boil. Substitute the hot apricots for water and instant coffee. Add 2 teaspoons lemon juice: prepare as directed, above.

Milk-Free
Egg-Free

Blueberry Sherbet

In a small bowl, sprinkle 2 teaspoons unflavored gelatin on ⅓ cup water to soften. In a medium saucepan, simmer ¼ cup granulated sugar with ⅓ cup water for 5 minutes: stir in gelatin mixture. Put one 10-ounce package frozen unsweetened whole blueberries into electric blender jar: add sugar-gelatin mixture: blend 2 minutes. Strain to remove pulp. Stir together strained juice, ¼ cup light corn syrup, and 3 tablespoons lemon juice. Pour mixture into ice-cube tray (Keep one just for this use) and fit with divider. Freeze 5 to 6 hours. Just before serving, place sherbet cubes and ⅓ cup water in blender: blend until smooth. Serve immediately. Makes 4 to 6 servings.

Ruby Ice

At least 5 hours before serving:

Press two 10-ounce packages thawed frozen raspberries through a sieve and discard seeds. In a medium bowl, beat 2 egg whites until soft peaks form. Slowly add $\frac{1}{4}$ cup granulated sugar, continuing to beat until stiff peaks form. Fold raspberry puree into this meringue. Freeze, stirring occasionally, until consistency of soft sherbet. Serve in chilled dishes. Makes 4 to 6 servings.

Homemade Strawberry Ice Cream

This is a great treat for a child on a milk-free diet. Make one quarter of this recipe to keep in freezer tray in your refrigerator.

> sugar
> 4 c. non-dairy frozen creamer
> 1 tsp. salt
> 1½ pts. strawberries, hulled
> 2 tbsp. lemon juice
> ¼ tsp. red food color
> 6 tbsp. all-purpose flour
> 6 eggs
> 4 c. non-dairy frozen creamer
> 2 to 3 lb. rock salt (about 3 c.)
> about 20 lb. cracked ice

Early in day or up to one month before serving:

In 4-quart, heavy saucepan, with spoon combine 2 cups sugar, flour and salt. In medium bowl, with hand beater or wire whisk, beat milk and eggs until well-blended; stir into sugar mixture until smooth. Cook over low heat, stirring constantly until mixture thickens and coats spoon, about 30 to 45 minutes. Cover surface of egg mixture with waxed paper and refrigerate until well-chilled, about 2 hours. Prepare strawberry mixture: in medium bowl, with potato masher or back of spoon, crush strawberries. Stir in lemon juice and 1 cup sugar; let stand about 1 hour. In 6-quart ice cream freezer can, stir well-cooled egg mixture, strawberry mixture, non-dairy frozen creamer, and red food color. Place dasher in can: cover and place can in freezer bucket: attach motor or hand crank: add 2 cups water to bucket. Fill bucket half full with ice: sprinkle with about $\frac{1}{4}$ cup rock salt. Add about an inch of ice and $\frac{1}{4}$ cup rock salt: repeat thin layers of ice and salt until about an inch below can lid. Freeze according to manufacturer's directions, adding more ice and salt as needed. It will take about 35 to 45 minutes to freeze. After freezing, ice cream will be soft. Remove motor, wiping lid carefully before removing. Remove dasher and, with spoon, pack down ice cream. Cover opening of can with waxed paper, plastic wrap, or foil. Replace lid and put cork in hole in center: add more ice and salt to cover lid. Let ice cream stand to harden, about 2 to 3 hours, adding more ice and salt as needed. (Or, place ice cream in a home freezer to harden, about 2 to 3 hours.) Makes about 4 quarts or 16 servings.

VANILLA: Prepare egg mixture as above: omit strawberry mixture. In 4 to 6 quart freezer can, combine egg mixture, non-dairy frozen creamer and 3 tablespoons vanilla extract: freeze as above. (If using 4-5 quart freezer can, do not add 2 cups water to bucket.) Makes about 3 quarts or 12 servings.

CHOCOLATE: Prepare egg mixture as above: omit 1 cup non-dairy frozen creamer. While mixture is cooling, in 1-quart saucepan over low heat, melt 8 squares unsweetened chocolate: stir in $\frac{3}{4}$ cup sugar and 1 cup hot water until blended: chill. In 4 to 6 quart freezer can, combine egg mixture, chocolate mixture, non-dairy frozen creamer, and 3 tablespoons vanilla extract: freeze as above. (If using 4 to 5 quart freezer can, do not add 2 cups water to bucket.) Makes about 3 quarts or 12 servings.

Milk-Free
Egg-Free

Popcorn Balls*

5 qts. popped corn
1½ c. water
½ c. light corn syrup
1 tsp. vanilla
2 c. sugar
½ tsp. salt
1 tsp. vinegar
colored sugar

Keep popcorn hot and crisp in slow oven (300°). Grease sides of saucepan and combine in it sugar, water, salt, corn syrup and vinegar. Cook to hard-ball stage. Add vanilla. Pour slowly over hot popped corn, mixing well to coat every kernel. Press into balls with greased hands. May be coated with colored sugar.

Milk-Free
Egg-Free

Pulled Molasses Mint Taffy*

In a 3-quart saucepan, mix 2 cups light molasses and 2 teaspoons white vinegar. Cook, gently stirring, to 260° F. on candy thermometer, or until a little mixture dropped into cold water becomes brittle. Remove from heat. Add 1½ tablespoons hydrogenated shortening, ⅛ teaspoon salt and ½ teaspoon baking soda. Stir until foaming stops: pour into greased 12 × 8 × 2-inch pan. When candy is cool enough to pull, drop 7 drops peppermint extract into center. Lift corners: draw to center: press together. Pull, using thumbs and fingers: fold. Repeat until light in color and quite firm. Pull into 2 long ropes, ¾-inch thick: twist. With scissors (dip often into hot water), cut into 1-inch pieces: wrap at once in waxed paper, plastic wrap, or foil. Makes about 6½ dozen pieces.

---

*Reprinted with permission from Allergy Information Association, Weston, Ontario, Canada.

CHAPTER 6

MEATS

MEAT WILL PROBABLY be in a milk-free diet at least twice a day and often three times. Do watch out for cold cuts, however, for many contain milk products. Try Kosher specialty stores.

Creamed on Toast

Make white sauce using cream substitute to replace the milk and milk-free margarine to replace the butter.

VARIATIONS:

Chipped Beef—good with sherry added to the sauce in small amounts.

Chicken á la King—sherry cream sauce, chicken pieces, 1 tbsp. chopped onion, sautéed, ½ cup mushrooms.

Lobster Newburg—sherry sauce-stir in 1 tbsp. sherry, 1½ cups cooked lobster meat and 1 tsp. paprika.

Creamed Eggs—make sauce. Add 1 tsp. mustard and 4 hard-boiled eggs, sliced.

Deviled Ham—Chop or grind ham, 1 tsp. minced pickle or pickle relish, 1 tsp. minced parsley, may add ½ tsp. Worchestershire sauce.

Tuna Souffle*

3 tbsp. shortening (milk-free)
2 tbsp. diced green pepper
2 tbsp. minced onion
2½ tbsp. flour
1 tsp. salt
1 5½ or 7- oz. can tuna, drained and flaked
4 eggs, separated
1 tbsp. lemon juice

*Reprinted with permission from Allergy Information Association, Weston, Ontario, Canada.

In medium saucepan melt shortening (milk-free) over low heat; in it sauté pepper and onion about 5 minutes. Stir in flour and cook, stirring, about 1 minute. Add water: cook, stirring constantly, until thickened. Stir in salt, lemon juice and tuna. Add egg yolks, blend well. In large bowl beat whites until stiff but not dry. Carefully fold in tuna mixture, then pour into ungreased 1½-quart casserole or souffle dish. Bake in 350° oven about 1 hour. Serve immediately. Yield: 4 servings.

VARIATION: salmon.

Milk-Free
Egg-Free

Johnny Mazetti

1 lb. ground pork
1 c. chopped green pepper
2 c. chopped onions
1 c. chopped celery
1/3 c. chopped stuffed olives
1 can (4 oz.) sliced mushrooms with liquid
1 can (10½ oz.) condensed tomato paste
1 can (8 oz.) tomato sauce
1 can (8 oz.) meatless tomato-mushroom sauce
2 lb. broad noodles
milk-free cracker crumbs
3 lb. ground beef
2 tsp. salt
½ c. oil

In a large skillet, sauté peppers, celery, onion and ground meats in hot oil. Add salt. Reduce heat. Add olives, mushrooms and tomatoes. Cook 5 minutes. Cook noodles following box directions. Drain. Turn into a 14 × 10 × 2½-inch pan. Add meat sauce and gently stir until well mixed. Sprinkle milk-free cracker crumbs on top. Bake at 350° for 35 minutes. Delicious. Freezes well. Can divide into three casseroles, serving 5-6 each. Yield: 16-18 portions.

Spaghetti Sauce for 25

2 lb. ground beef
3 green peppers
1 lb. mushrooms, sliced
3 cans water
1 small red hot pepper
salt
¼ lb. grated Parmesan cheese*, separately
2 cloves garlic, minced
1 lb. ground pork
2 lb. onions
3 cans Italian tomato paste
3 #2 cans tomatoes
¾ c. salad oil
3 lb. spaghetti

Sauté onions, garlic and green pepper in oil for 20 minutes. Add meat and break it into small pieces as it cooks. Cook the meats with onion, garlic and green pepper for ½ hour. Add tomato paste diluted with the cans of water and the tomatoes. Add red pepper broken into small pieces and the salt. Simmer 1 to 2 hours until the sauce has thickened. Stir occasionally to keep the sauce from stocking. Boil the spaghetti 10 minutes in salted water. Drain. Pour boiling water over it. Mix sauce and spaghetti or serve spaghetti, sauce and cheese separately, mixing each serving. Always put spaghetti in a hot dish or on a hot platter and have the serving plates warmed.

---

*Cheese is listed only for those of the 20-25 who are not on a milk-free diet. Thus it is served separately to be added individually.

Meat Balls

4 lb. ground beef
½ c. grated onion
2 c. Ritz® or milk-free fine cracker crumbs
salt, pepper, garlic salt
1 tsp. oregano
1 lb. ground pork
½ c. water
finely chopped parsley

Moisten cracker crumbs with water, add to rest of ingredients and mix thoroughly. Shape into meatballs. Brown in oil. Pour off fat and serve with spaghetti and cheese-free sauce. For spaghetti, this serves 15-20 people—divide by 4 for family of 3 or 4.

Sloppy Joes

½ c. minced onion
2 tbsp. milk-free margarine
1½ lb. ground beef
2-4 tbsp. chili sauce or catsup
½ c. chopped green peppers
½ c. chopped mushrooms
salt to taste

Sauté the onion and green pepper in the milk-free margarine until tender. Add the meat and cook until lightly browned, stirring with a fork. Add mushrooms, chili sauce and seasoning. Cook, uncovered, for five minutes. Serve on lightly toasted, milk-free buns.

Special Meat Loaf for 20

Divide by 4 to serve an ordinary family.

> 5 lbs. ground beef (½ lb. ground veal if available—optional)
> 2 c. milk-free cracker crumbs or corn flakes
> 3 eggs, well beaten
> ½ c. non-dairy frozen creamer
> 1 c. catsup or chili sauce (I prefer chili sauce)
> ½ c. pepper relish or pickle relish (optional)
> cloves
> 1 lb. ground pork
> 3 onions, grated (optional)

Combine beef and pork. Mix liquid ingredients and pour over meat. Sprinkle milk-free cracker crumbs and seasoning over all and mix. Shape into 3 loaves. Place on heavy foil on wire rack in baking pan. Pierce the foil with fork in several places so the fat can drain into bottom pan. Stud the loaves with cloves as for baked ham for special flavor. Bake at 375° for 30 minutes with a piece of foil laid loosely over the top. Remove foil and bake 15-20 minutes more.

Milk-Free
Egg-Free

Chicken Pie for 20

> 3 large chickens
> onion
> carrot
> salt, pepper, oregano
> celery
> 6 c. chicken broth (save from boiling)

Boil chickens until tender with salt, pepper, oregano, and a little onion, celery, and carrot. Save 6 cups of chicken broth from boiling. Remove bones and skin and cut chicken into large bite-size pieces. Thicken broth with flour, cook until consistency of gravy. May moisten flour with non-dairy frozen creamer before adding to broth. Season as desired (I use a little lemon-garlic flavor) . Add chicken meat and three packages of frozen peas and carrots. Cover with pie crust. Bake 350° for 50 minutes or until brown and bubbly.

Milk-Free
Egg-Free

Beef Casserole Stew

Milk-free, egg-free and good

2½ lb. beef, chuck or round
salt and pepper to taste
1 tbsp. flour
2 carrots, diced
1 c. strained tomatoes
2 tbsp. oil
1 small onion, sliced
1 bay leaf

Season meat, cut into pieces, dust with flour. Heat fat in a skillet and brown the meat in it on all sides. Place meat in casserole, add other ingredients, cover and simmer in a slow oven at 300° until tender, about 2½ hours. Serve hot with mashed, baked or boiled potatoes.

Milk-Free
Egg-Free

Oven Barbecued Short Ribs

For the short rib fans

2-3 lb. beef short ribs
1 can (8 oz.) tomato sauce
2 tbsp. chopped onion
2 tbsp. vinegar
dash of cayenne pepper
½ c. red wine vinegar
1½ tsp. salt
1 tbsp. prepared mustard

Rub hot Dutch oven with some of the fat from the ribs: brown ribs slowly on all sides. Drain off fat. Combine other ingredients: pour over the ribs. Cover, bake in slow oven, 300°, for 1½-2 hours or until meat is tender.

Milk-Free
Egg-Free

Beef Casserole*

1½ lb. ground chuck
1 green pepper, chopped
1 c. celery, chopped
½ tsp. salt
1 28-oz. can of tomatoes
6 oz. fine noodles (use rice vermicelli for gluten-free diets)
grated cheese (omit for milk-free diets and use crumb topping)
¾ lb. sliced mushrooms (or 1 10-oz. can)
1 pkg. dried onion soup mix
1 tsp. Worcestershire sauce
pinch of thyme

Sauté beef, mushrooms, pepper and celery in oil. Add tomatoes, soup mix, Worcestershire sauce, salt and thyme. Cook until excess moisture has gone. Cook rice vermicelli or noodles, drain well, and add to meat mixture. Put in casserole, adding milk-free crumb topping. Heat in 350° oven for ½ to ¾ hour. If desired, omit mushrooms, celery and tomatoes, and substitute stuffed olives, canned corn niblets and your favorite soup. Serves 12.

Salisbury Steak Casserole†

2 lb. lean beef ground
pepper to taste
1 egg
barbecue sauce
1½ tsp. salt
2 tbsp. finely chopped onion
2 tbsp. milk-free margarine

---

*Reprinted with permission from Allergy Information Association, Weston, Ontario, Canada.
†Reprinted with permission from Allergy Information Association, Weston. Ontario, Canada.

Mix beef, salt, pepper, onion and egg thoroughly but lightly. Grease a good-sized shallow casserole, mold the meat mixture into an oval resembling a small loaf of french bread, and put in center of casserole. Brush with barbecue sauce and bake in a 450° oven for 10 minutes. Reduce heat to 325° and bake 25-35 minutes longer. Brush with barbecue sauce at least twice during baking. Serve with sautéed mushrooms and little onions. Yield: 6 servings.

Meat Loaf

2 lb. chuck
1 slice bread wet with milk-substitute, squeeze & crumble
seasoning to taste
1 egg
bacon strips

Mix ingredients. Form into loaf shape. Put bacon strips on grill. Place meat loaf on it. Add bacon and grill slowly.

Milk-Free
Egg-Free

Rice-Burger Casserole*

1 lb. ground beef
¼ c. diced bacon (4 slices)
2 tbsp. parsley flakes
1 tbsp. chopped green pepper
1 egg, unbeaten
½ tsp. salt
4 c. seasoned, cooked long-grain rice
1 tbsp. gluten-free soya sauce
2 tbsp. tomato ketchup
2 tbsp. margarine
¼ lb. ground pork
1 tbsp. finely chopped onion
1 tsp. seasoning salt
¼ tsp. pepper
¼ c. water

*Reprinted with permission from Allergy Information Association, Weston, Ontario, Canada.

Mix thoroughly in medium-sized bowl the beef, pork, bacon, parsley flakes, onion, celery, green pepper, egg, seasoning salt, salt and pepper. Butter a large-sized casserole dish and spread warm cooked rice over the bottom, making a layer with approximately 3 cups of the rice. Cover rice with meat mixture, flattening it fairly well. On top of meat, sprinkle soya sauce, ketchup and water mixed. Make another layer on top of meat with remaining rice. Cover and bake in moderate oven at 375° for 30 minutes. Remove casserole dish from oven, spread milk-free margarine over top layer of rice and replace the cover. Allow casserole to bake for ten minutes longer at 350°. Yield: 6 to 8 servings.

Sweet-Sour Meat Balls*

Preparation time, 35 minutes including cooking time, 20 minutes Yield: 6 servings.

> 1 lb. ground beef
> ½ c. finely chopped almonds
> 1 tsp. salt
> 2 eggs, slightly beaten
> cooking oil
> ¾ c. finely diced celery
> 2 tbsp. minced onion
> cornstarch
> hot rice

SAUCE:

> ½ c. sugar
> 1 c. boiling water
> 2 chicken bouillon cubes
> ½ c. pineapple juice
> 3 tbsp. cornstarch
> ½ c. vinegar
> 2 tsp. soy sauce
> 1 c. pineapple chunks
> 1 green pepper cut in thin strips

---

*Reprinted with permission from Allergy Information Association, Weston, Ontario, Canada.

Mix together the first 7 ingredients and shape into small meat balls less than one inch in diameter. Roll them in cornstarch. Brown slowly in hot oil, cooking about 15 minutes. Turn frequently. Make sauce by mixing sugar and cornstarch in a saucepan. Dissolve bouillon cubes in boiling water and stir into sugar-cornstarch along with vinegar, soy sauce and pineapple juice. Stir, cooking until sauce is smooth and slightly thickened. Add green pepper and pineapple. Heat to serving temperature. Pour over meat balls. Serve on hot rice. *(The meat balls and sauce may be frozen, if desired.)*

Oven Meat Balls*

Meat balls and sauce all done in the same pan

> 1 lb. lean ground beef
> 1/3 c. dry bread crumbs (milk-free)
> 1 tbsp. dried parsley flakes
> pepper and salt to taste
> 2 tbsp. grated onion
> 2 tbsp. oil
> 2 tbsp. cornstarch
> ½ tsp. salt
> ½ c. mayonnaise
> 1 egg
> 1/3 c. water or beef broth
> 1½ c. Coffee Rich
> 2 tsp. Worcestershire sauce
> 1 pkg. Farm Rich Foods® Mushrooms

Preheat oven to 400°. Mix beef, bread crumbs, eggs, seasonings and water together and form into 12 meat balls. Brush meat balls with oil. Bake in 400° oven for 30 minutes. Pour off excess fat. Combine Coffee Rich, corn starch, seasoning, frozen mushrooms and sour cream. Pour over meat balls. Return to 400° oven for 15 minutes.

Yield: 4 servings.

Preparation Time: 50 minutes.

*Reprinted with permission from Rich Products Corp., P.O. Box 245, 1145 Niagara St., Buffalo, N.Y.

Stuffed Cabbage in Tomato Sauce*

        1 lb. lean ground beef
        1 small chopped onion
        1 tsp. each caraway seed (optional) and salt
        1 egg
        1 c. cooked rice
        ¼ tsp. pepper

Mix above ingredients. Trim off thickest part of stem from 12 cabbage leaves. Divide meat into 12 portions, wrap each in a leaf, fasten with wooden picks. Brown cabbage rolls in cooking oil. Add contents of two 8-oz. cans tomato sauce, and ¼ cup water. Cover, cook slowly about 40 minutes. Yield: 6 servings.

Milk-Free
Egg-Free

Grandmother's Kettle Stew

            cubed beef—lean
            potatoes—peeled
            ½ c. red wine (optional)
            carrots—peeled
            flour
            kitchen bouquet

Brown beef cubes in stew kettle or electric frypan. Add water to cover well and ½ cup red wine. Cook at low heat so it just simmers for 2½ to 3 hours. May add more water from time to time if necessary, usually not. During last half hour, add vegetables. Just before serving pour off liquid, thicken it with flour, add ⅛ to ¼ tsp. of Kitchen Bouquet® and pour over meat and vegetables. (May cool and refrigerate at this point, keeps 2 to 3 days) Heat and serve hot with salad.

VARIATIONS: peas, mushrooms, celery or onions may be added according to your taste. Try it plain first.

---

*Reprinted with permission from Allergy Information Association, Weston, Ontario, Canada.

Milk-Free
Egg-Free

Chicken Divan

1 pkg. (10 oz.) frozen asparagus spears
3 tbsp. milk-free margarine
3 tbsp. flour
1 can (2 oz.) mushroom stems and pieces
salt and pepper
8 slices (1 lb.) cooked chicken or turkey
2 tbsp. milk-free bread crumbs
1 c. chicken broth
2 tbsp. chopped parsley

Cook asparagus spears. Mix milk-free margarine and flour in saucepan. Cook 1 minute, stirring constantly. Blend in chicken broth. Cook and stir over medium heat until thick. Stir in mushrooms and liquid. Season to taste with salt and pepper. In a shallow baking pan or 4 individual casseroles, place asparagus spears. Cover with sliced chicken or turkey, then with sauce. Top with parsley and crumbs. Bake at 375° for 15 to 25 minutes or until bubbly. Makes 4 servings.

Milk-Free
Egg-Free

Hacienda Chicken

½ c. sliced Spanish Green Olives
½ c. chopped onion
1 2½-oz. can sliced mushrooms
1 tbsp. chopped parsley
1 cut-up stewing chicken
1 16-oz. can tomatoes
1 clove
¼ tsp. pepper
1 c. water
1 tbsp. salt
3 tbsp. milk-free margarine
½ c. chopped green pepper
1 tsp. paprika
1 c. rice

Melt margarine in heavy skillet. Add onion and cook until lightly browned. Add tomatoes, water, green pepper, mushrooms and liquid, clove, parsley, paprika, salt and pepper. Cut chicken into serving pieces and add to ingredients in kettle. Cover. Bring to boil, reduce heat and simmer for 1 hour. Add rice and olives and continue cooking until rice is done and chicken is tender (approximately one hour). Makes 6 servings.

Milk-Free
Egg-Free

Grilled, Herbed Chicken Breasts

    4 lg. chicken breasts
    6 tbsp. (¾ stick) milk-free margarine
    2 tbsp. chopped fresh dill
    1 tbsp. lemon juice
    ¼ c. chopped parsley
    1 c. soft, fine milk-free bread crumbs
    salt, freshly ground black pepper
    melted milk-free margarine
    2 tbsp. onion, freshly chopped

Halve the breasts, removing the bone. Cut through the thickest part of each half-breast to form a pocket. Season lightly with salt and pepper. Cream the margarine. Add the parsley, dill, onion and lemon juice. Mix well and stir in the bread crumbs. Fill the pockets with the mixture and skewer to close. Brush with melted margarine and grill over hot coals, turning to brown all sides. Cooking time will be about twenty minutes. Yield: 8 servings.

Milk-Free
Egg-Free

Chicken Rosemary

    1 tsp. rosemary, finely crushed
    1 2½-3 lb. ready-to-cook, broiler-fryer chicken, cut up
    salt and pepper
    2 tbsp. fat
    1 3-oz. can (2/3 c.) broiled, sliced mushrooms, drained
    1/3 c. sauterne

Mix rosemary and sauterne: let stand several hours at room temperature. Lightly season chicken with salt and pepper: brown slowly in hot fat. Add sauterne mixture. Cover: simmer 45 minutes or until chicken is tender. Add mushrooms, heat through. Remove chicken to hot platter. Stir 2 tablespoons additional sauterne into pan drippings, if desired. Serve sauce over chicken. Makes 4 servings.

Milk-Free
Egg-Free

Chicken Legs Grilled in Foil

> ready-to-cook chicken legs
> milk-free margarine
> chopped onion or chives
> salt & pepper to taste

Wrap each leg securely in foil with a pat of margarine, a teaspoon of chopped onion or chopped chives, and salt and pepper to taste. Grill the packages over hot coals, turning once. Cooking time will be about 40 minutes.

Milk-Free
Egg-Free

Roast Chicken Casserole

5 lb. roasting chicken, disjointed
½ tsp. freshly ground black pepper
1 tsp. paprika
12 mushroom caps
2½ tsp. salt
4 tbsp. rendered chicken fat or milk-free margarine
3 potatoes, peeled and quartered
3 carrots, quartered
12 small white onions
½ c. chicken broth
1 clove garlic, minced
2 tbsp. chopped parsley

Mix together the salt, pepper, garlic and paprika, rub into the chicken. Melt the fat or margarine in a casserole: brown the chicken in it. Add the onions and potatoes and brown lightly. Add the mushrooms, carrots and broth. Cover and cook over low heat 45 minutes or until chicken is tender. To serve, remove cover and sprinkle with the parsley. Serves 4-6.

Chicken Tahitian

> 3 pkg. Swanson Baked Breast of Chicken®
> 4 c. cooked rice
> 6-oz. can pineapple concentrate, thawed
> ½ c. macadamia nuts
> 2 tbsp. lemon juice
> 2 avocados, peeled, sliced (¾" slices)
> ¼ tsp. ginger
> ½ c. milk-free margarine
> 6 orange slices

Prepare Swanson Baked Breast of Chicken according to package direction. Meanwhile, prepare rice. In small saucepan, melt margarine on low temperature. Then slowly add the thawed pineapple concentrate, lemon juice and ginger. Combine thoroughly and let simmer for 12-15 minutes. To serve: place mound of rice in center of large serving platter. Arrange chicken breasts around outer edge of rice. Between chicken breasts, alternately arrange avocado slices and orange slices. Spoon 2 tablespoons of the pineapple glaze over each chicken breast. Add the macadamia nuts to the remainder of glaze in the saucepan, then remove from glaze and place on rice in center of platter. Place platter in 400° oven for 10-15 minutes and serve piping hot. Heat remaining gravy in saucepan and spoon over rice when served.

Milk-Free
Egg-Free

Savory Chicken Rice Bake

1 c. uncooked long grain rice
½ c. chopped onion
1 can beef broth
¼ tsp. rosemary
½ c. water
¼ tsp. oregano
1 c. chopped celery
½ tsp. monosodium glutamate
1 clove garlic, minced
½ tsp. salt
3 chicken breasts, boned and halved

Toast rice in moderate oven (350°) about 25 minutes or till golden brown. Dredge chicken in mixture of flour, salt and pepper, brown in ¼ c. hot fat. Remove chicken from skillet: add onion and garlic, cook until onion is tender. Stir in rice and remaining ingredients: transfer to an 11 × 7 × 1½-inch baking dish. Top with chicken breasts. Cover tightly with foil, bake at 350° for 50 minutes or until chicken is done and rice is tender. Sprinkle with chopped parsley and sliced toasted almonds if desired.

Milk-Free
Egg-Free

Oven Sauteéd Chicken*

Chicken in a rich creamy sauce

3 tbsp. vegetable oil
pepper and salt
dried parsley flakes
1 tbsp. cornstarch
1 tsp. Worcestershire sauce
1 6-oz. pkg. Farm Rich Foods Mushrooms
2½-3 lb. cut-up fryer
celery and garlic salt
1 c. Coffee Rich
1 tsp. paprika

*Reprinted with permission from Rich Products Corp., P.O. Box 245, 1145 Niagara St., Buffalo, N.Y.

Preheat oven to 400°. Brush chicken with oil, place in baking dish. Sprinkle seasonings on chicken in amounts desired. Bake in 400° oven 45 minutes. Combine Coffee Rich, cornstarch, paprika and Worcestershire sauce and stir with wire whip until blended. Add frozen mushrooms to sauce and pour over chicken. Return chicken to 400° oven, bake 10-15 minutes longer.
Yield: 4 servings.
Preparation time: 1 hour.

Note: *Chicken may be prepared on top of range. Brown in oil, add seasonings and cook covered until chicken is tender (about 30 minutes). Add sauce and heat through. If a crusty brown is desired, place under broiler 3-5 minutes before serving.*

Milk-Free
Egg-Free

Baked Ham with Spicy Currant Glaze*

Ham
Spicy Currant Glaze (recipe below)
canned peach halves (optional)
French's Whole Cloves®

Bake ham according to instructions on wrapper. Remove from oven 20 to 30 minutes before end of cooking time. Carefully remove any rind and score in diamond or square design. Stud with French's Whole Cloves. Spoon about half the glaze over ham and continue baking 20 to 30 minutes, spoon remaining glaze several times. Note: *For a delicious, attractive garnish, heat canned peach halves in oven with ham for about 10 minutes, spooning some of the glaze over them.*

---

*Reprinted with permission from R.T. French advertisement in newspaper.

Spicy Currant Glaze

1 c. currant jelly
¼ c. French's prepared mustard
½ tsp. French's Cloves
few drops French's Red Food Color®
½ c. brown sugar
½ tsp. French's Cinnamon®

Combine all ingredients and heat, stirring occasionally, until mixture boils and jelly is melted.

Milk-Free
Egg-Free

Hawaiian Hash*

3 c. diced ham
3 c. diced sweet potatoes (canned or cooked)
1 can (13¼ oz.) pineapple chunks or
    4 slices pineapple plus syrup
½ c. orange juice, approximately
6 tbsp. brown sugar
4 tbsp. milk-free margarine
3 tbsp. French's Mustard with Onion Bits®
French's Cinnamon
1 tbsp. cornstarch
½ tsp. salt

Mix together ham and sweet potatoes in greased shallow 1½-quart baking dish. Drain syrup from pineapple: add orange juice to make 1 cup liquid. In small saucepan, blend together cornstarch and pineapple-orange juice. Add 2 tablespoons of the brown sugar, salt and 2 tablespoons milk-free margarine. Bring to a boil: reduce heat and cook until slightly thickened, stirring constantly. When thickened, stir in mustard: pour over ham and sweet potatoes. Bake in 350° oven for 30 minutes or until bubbly hot. Meanwhile, using two knives or a pastry blender, but 2 tablespoons milk-free margarine into remaining brown sugar until mixture

*Reprinted with permission from R.T. French advertisement in newspaper.

is crumbly. When ham mixture is heated through, remove from oven and top with pineapple chunks or slices. Spoon brown sugar-margarine evenly over pineapple and ham mixture: sprinkle with cinnamon. Broil 5-7 minutes or until pineapple is lightly browned. Yield: 5-6 servings.

Ham 'n Macaroni Salad*

2 c. uncooked elbow macaroni
1 envelope French's Chili-O Mix®
1 c. mayonnaise
2 c. diced celery
½ c. sweet pickle relish, drained
2 c. diced ham
lettuce
tomato wedges and
sliced hardboiled eggs if desired

Cook macaroni as directed on the package: drain well. Stir contents of envelope of Chili-O mix into mayonnaise, add to hot, drained macaroni, stirring well. Chill. Add ham, celery and pickle relish. Serve on lettuce leaves, garnished with tomatoes and hard-boiled eggs. 6-8 servings.

Ham Ala Rich†

So easy you won't even know you are cooking

½ c. bottled barbeque sauce
¼ c. Coffee Rich
¾-1 lb. ham slice
1 tsp. sugar

Preheat oven to 375°. Combine barbeque sauce, Coffee Rich and sugar. Place ham slice in baking dish, pour sauce over. Bake in 375° oven for 20 minutes.
Yield: 3-4 servings.
Preparation time: 20 minutes.

---

*Reprinted with permission from R.T. French advertisement in newspaper.
†Reprinted with permission from Rich Products Corp., P.O. Box 245, 1145 Niagara St., Buffalo, N.Y.

Upside Down Pineapple Ham Loaf

A good meat stretcher, very tasty

> 7 c. ground cooked ham
> 1 lb. beef, round ground
> 4 c. day old, milk-free bread crumbs
> 1 tsp. salt
> 2 eggs, slightly beaten
> 4 medium celery stalks, finely chopped
> 1½ c. milk-substitute
> ¼ c. chopped parsley
> 5 canned pineapple slices and maraschino cherries
> 1 lb. veal shoulder, ground
> ½ tsp. poultry seasoning
> ½ tsp. pepper
> ½ c. catsup
> 2 medium onions, finely chopped (¾ c.)
> ½ c. brown sugar, packed

Combine all ingredients in mixing bowl except brown sugar, pineapple and cherries. Sprinkle brown sugar in bottom of 10″ angel food cake pan. Arrange cherries and pineapple on top of sugar. Press meat mixture around pineapple, then pat remainder on top. Bake at 350° for 1½ hours. When done, pour off and save drippings. Invert on platter, pineapple side up. Lift off pan. Spoon drippings over top. Serves 12-16.

Milk-Free
Egg-Free

Lamb with Rice*

> 3 tbsp. rice flour
> 1 c. hot water
> 1½ c. hot cooked rice
> 2 tbsp. lamb drippings
> ½ tsp. salt

Brown rice flour in drippings. Add water and salt. Cook and stir until thick and smooth. Add lamb and heat thoroughly. Serve over rice. Yield: 3 servings.

---

*Reprinted with permission from Allergy Information Association, Weston, Ontario, Canada.

Milk-Free
Egg-Free

Lamb Stew†

½ lb. lamb, cut for stew
¾ tsp. salt
1¼ c. hot water
1½ c. diced, pared sweet potatoes
1 tbsp. rice flour
1 tbsp. lamb drippings
1 tbsp. rice flour

Boil lamb in mixture of flour and salt. Brown in hot drippings. Add water. Cover, simmer 1 hour. Add potatoes, cover, and cook 25 minutes longer or until tender. Make gravy with liquid and 1 tablespoon rice flour. Yield: 3 servings.

Milk-Free
Egg-Free

Breaded Veal Steak

4 (5 oz. each) cubed veal steaks
2 tbsp. fine, dry milk-free bread crumbs
salt and pepper
3 tbsp. milk-free margarine

Dredge steak in crumbs seasoned with salt and pepper. Sauté slowly in milk-free margarine until browned on one side. Turn and brown the other side, allowing about 5 to 7 minutes per steak. Makes 4 servings.

---

†Reprinted with permission from Allergy Information Association, Weston, Ontario, Canada.

Milk-Free
Egg-Free

Fish Provencale

1 tbsp. milk-free margarine
1 very small onion, minced
½ clove garlic, minced
½ can sliced mushrooms, drained
pinch thyme
dash pepper
¼ c. white wine
1 tbsp. chopped parsley
1 tbsp. flour
¼ tsp. salt
½ c. canned tomatoes, chopped
½ lb. frozen haddock fillets
1 tbsp. milk-free margarine

In skillet melt milk-free margarine and in it sauté onion and garlic over medium heat for 3 minutes. Add mushrooms, thyme, salt, pepper, tomatoes and white wine. Place frozen fillets in center of skillet and bring liquid to a boil. Sprinkle with parsley, cover tightly, and simmer for 20 minutes. Uncover and break fish into small pieces with a fork. Mix soft butter and flour to a smooth paste and stir into liquid in skillet, bit by bit. Cook, stirring 3 minutes longer. Serve hot on toast or with cooked rice.

Milk-Free
Egg-Free

Oven Fried Fish

2 small dressed fish
1 tsp. salt
1/3 c. fine dry milk-free bread crumbs
dash cayenne
1/3 c. milk-substitute
1 tsp. paprika
2 tbsp. melted milk-free margarine or bacon drippings

Wipe fish with a damp paper towel. In a flat dish, combine milk substitute and salt. On piece of waxed paper, mix bread crumbs, paprika and cayenne. Dip fish in milk-substitute and roll in crumbs. Place fish in well-greased baking dish. Pour melted fat over fish. Bake in a preheated 500° oven on shelf near top of oven for 10-12 minutes, or until fish flakes easily when tested with a fork. Serve on warm serving plates garnished with lemon wedge. Buttered parsley potatoes and asparagus make excellent vegetable accompaniments.

Avocado Seafood Salad

1 med. avocado
1 c. flaked lobster meat or Alaska King Crab Meat
1/3 c. mayonnaise
2 tbsp. minced gherkins or dill pickle
1/8 tsp. dry mustard
1 tsp. lemon juice or tarragon vinegar
2 green onions, minced
1 tbsp. minced parsley
salt and pepper to taste

Cut avocado in half lengthwise and remove peel and seed. Combine remaining ingredients with salt and pepper to taste. Fill avocado halves with the seafood mixture. If desired, garnish each serving with water cress and stuffed olives.

Salmon Mousse

2 env. plain gelatin
1 chicken bouillon cube
1 1-lb. can salmon
few drops tabasco
1/2 c. mayonnaise
2 tbsp. cold water
1 c. boiling water
1 tsp. lemon juice
1/4 tsp. salt or to taste
1/2 c. cream substitute, whipped

Soften 1 envelope of the gelatin in cold water for 5 minutes. Dissolve bouillon cube in boiling water, add to gelatin, and stir until gelatin is thoroughly dissolved. Pour into bottom of a 1-quart mold and chill until set. Drain liquid from salmon into measuring cup and add water to make a total of ½ cup liquid. Soften remaining envelope of gelatin in this mixture for 5 minutes, then set cup into pan containing simmering water and stir until gelatin is thoroughly dissolved. Flake salmon into a bowl and beat in lemon juice, tabasco and salt. Continue to beat while gradually adding the dissolved gelatin. Use your electric beater for this and mix until salmon is smooth and fluffy. Stir in mayonnaise and finally fold in the whipped cream. Pack the mousse into the aspic-coated pan and chill for 2 hours, or until ready to serve.

To serve: Run a knife around the inside edge of mold. Dip mold in and out of water, just hot to the hand, three times and invert mold over serving platter. Mold should lift cleanly away. Garnish with lettuce leaves and a hard-cooked egg.

Hot Chicken Supreme

Wonderful buffet main dish

> 2 c. cooked, cut-up chicken breasts (not too small)
> 1 c. chopped celery
> 1 c. cooked rice
> ¾ c. mayonnaise
> 2 cans water chestnuts, sliced
> 1 tbsp. minced onion
> 1 tbsp. lemon juice
> 1 c. chicken broth, thickened with paste made of 2½ tbsp. flour
>   with ¼ c. water (stir until smooth, then pour into the
>   chicken broth and heat, stirring until thick).
> 3 sliced hard-boiled eggs

Mix together and put into a greased casserole. Melt ½ lb. milk-free margarine and pour over. Add ½ cup cornflake crumbs, 1 package of sliced almonds. Mixture may be made ahead and refrigerated for a day or two at this point. Bake at 350° about 35-40 minutes. Serves 8-10.

FOR YEARS THERE WERE NO COMMERCIALLY offered stuffing bread that was labeled as to ingredients. Recently I have found several prepared bread cubes milk-free and a couple of boxed milk-free stuffing mixes.

Milk-Free
Egg-Free

Stuffing for Poultry

For 12-16 pound turkey

> 2 loaves milk-free bread
> 1 c. diced onion (may use 1 pkg. frozen diced onion)
> ¼ c. vegetable oil
> pepper
> 1 c. finely chopped celery
> salt
> garlic salt

Brown onion and celery in oil quickly. Pour over bread pieces and mix well. Season and let stand at least ½ hour. Mix again and stuff into cavities of bird.

Milk-Free
Egg-Free

Mushroom Bread Stuffing

> 1 can (2 oz.) mushrooms, stems and pieces
> ¼ c. finely chopped celery
> ¼ c. finely chopped onion
> 1 tsp. poultry seasoning
> 3 c. dry, milk-free bread cubes (about 8 slices)
> ¼ tsp. salt
> ⅛ tsp. pepper
> ¼ c. milk-free margarine

Drain mushrooms, reserving liquid. Saute celery, onion and mushrooms in milk-free margarine until tender. Add bread cubes, seasoning and mushroom liquid. Toss lightly. If a more moist dressing is desired, add a small amount of water. Makes 4 servings. For chops or Rock Cornish Hens.

S̶o MANY VARIETIES are available canned, frozen and fresh that few vegetable recipes are included. Please notice that straight vegetables meat and potatotes, and salads are all milk-free and egg-free and should make up the prime portion of a milk-free diet.

Beware of the fancier frozen vegetables with sauces, etc., for almost all contain butter or milk.

Potatoes With Mushrooms*

½ lb. fresh mushrooms, sliced or 4-oz. can mushrooms, drained
½ c. chopped onion
½ tsp. salt
1 envelope (5 servings) French's Mashed Potato®
French's paprika and parsley flakes
3 tbsp. milk-free margarine
⅛ tsp. French's pepper

Cook fresh mushrooms and onion in butter (milk-free margarine) until mushrooms are soft but not brown. Add salt and pepper. Prepare potatoes according to package directions, except omit butter. Add mushrooms to potatoes: sprinkle with paprika and parsley flakes. Yield: 5 servings

---

*Reprinted with permission from R.T. French Co. newspaper advertisement.

Mixed Vegetables (French Ratatouille)

1 med. eggplant
¼ c. vegetable oil
3 cloves (or less) crushed garlic
2 green peppers, cut into strips
4 med. zucchini, cut into squares
freshly ground black pepper
1 bay leaf
1 tbsp. salt
2 lg. onions, cut into rings
   or 1 tsp. garlic salt
¼ tsp. salt
2 med. tomatoes, cut into wedges
½ tsp. thyme
2 tbsp. parsley, finely chopped

Cut eggplant into thick slices and then into small pieces. Sprinkle with salt. Allow to stand 30 minutes, then rinse and pat dry on paper towels. Heat the oil in a large skillet or electric frying pan. Sauté onions and garlic for 2 minutes. Add green pepper and cook for 2 minutes. Add eggplant and cook over high heat for 3 minutes, stirring. Add zucchini and stir 3 more minutes. Add tomatoes, salt, pepper, thyme and bay leaf. Simmer uncovered for 40 minutes until all vegetables are tender. Remove bay leaf, garnish with parsley, and serve hot.

French Omelet*

A French touch to eggs that's very easy

For each serving:

1 egg
salt & pepper to taste
1 tbsp. Coffee Rich
1 tbsp. fat

---

*Reprinted with permission from Rich Products Corp., P.O. Box 245, 1145 Niagara St., Buffalo, N.Y.

Beat egg with Coffee Rich and seasonings until egg and white are mixed. Melt fat in omlet pan and pour in egg mixture. Cook slowly, keeping heat low. As under surface becomes set, start lifting it slightly with spatula to let uncooked portion flow underneath. When lightly browned on bottom, fold and turn onto hot serving dish.

Egg Yolk Omelet†

What to do with leftover egg yolks

> 10 egg yolks
> 10 tbsp. Coffee Rich (½ c. + 2 tbsp.)
> pepper
> 2 tbsp. milk-free margarine
> salt
> 1 tsp. baking powder

Beat egg yolks slightly, add Coffee Rich and beat until lemon colored. Add seasonings and baking powder. Melt fat in skillet, pour in eggs. Cook over low heat. As under-surface becomes set, start lifting it slightly with spatula to let uncooked portion flow underneath. When lightly browned, fold over and turn into hot platter. Yield: 4 servings. Preparation time: 10 minutes.

Note: Use Coffee Rich for making regular omelets, too.

Puffed Omelet*

Serve for breakfast, lunch or supper

For each serving:

> 2 eggs
> salt & pepper to taste
> ¼ c. Coffee Rich
> 1 tbsp. milk-free margarine

---

†Reprinted with permission from Rich Products Corp., P.O. Box 245, 1145 Niagara St., Buffalo, N.Y.
*Reprinted with permission from Rich Products Corp., P.O. Box 245, 1145 Niagara St., Buffalo, N.Y.

FILLING:
Your choice, sautéed mushrooms, bacon, cheese, jelly, catsup.

Separate eggs. Add Coffee Rich and seasonings to yolks. Beat until well-mixed. Beat the egg whites until stiff. Fold into the yolks. Melt milk-free margarine in 8-inch skillet, add eggs. Cook, loosening and lifting the edges until eggs are set but still moist on top. Spread the eggs with filling, reserving some for garnish. With a rubber spatula roll the omelet away from you and make the final roll by turning the omelet onto serving plate. Garnish the top with reserved filling.

Yield: 1 serving
Preparation time: 5 minutes.

Spinach With Bacon

Cook frozen chopped spinach as in directions. Add chopped bacon or imitation bacon bits and a dash of nutmeg.

San Antonio Spinach Pudding*

If you are a fan of spinach, this custard vegetable entree will become a favorite.

3 eggs
1 tbsp. grated onion
¼ tsp. pepper
1 c. Coffee Rich
½ tsp. salt
1 10-oz. package frozen chopped spinach or 1½ c. cooked, chopped spinach

Preheat oven to 350°.

Beat eggs until light and lemon colored. Blend in Coffee Rich and seasonings. Cook spinach until just tender and blend into Coffee Rich-egg mixture. Pour into buttered 1-quart casserole.

---

*Reprinted with permission from Rich Products Corp., P.O. Box 245, 1145 Niagara St., Buffalo, N.Y.

Bake in preheated 350° oven for 45 minutes or until set and silver knife comes out clean.

Yield: 4 servings

Preparation time: 50 minutes

Scalloped Tomatoes

12-14 oz. tomatoes, canned
¼ tsp. salt
¼ c. milk-free margarine, melted
½ c. boiling water
6 tbsp. brown sugar

Heat tomatoes, water, salt and sugar to boiling. Add 1 cup of milk-free fresh white bread crumbs. Place in a baking dish. Pour over this ¼ cup melted milk-free margarine. Add the tomato sauce and cover. Bake at 375° for 30 minutes.

Zucchini Italienne

4 c. zucchini cut in ¼-inch slices (1 lb.)
¼ c. water
1 med. onion, thinly sliced
3 tbsp. milk-free margarine
1 tbsp. dried parsley flakes
¼ tsp. leaf oregano
1 large tomato, peeled and thinly sliced
1/3 c. milk-free bread crumbs
½ tsp. salt

Place zucchini, water and salt in saucepan. Cover and cook over low heat about 10 minutes (zucchini should be firm). Drain. Sauté onion in milk-free margarine until tender. Stir in parsley and oregano. Layer zucchini, tomato slices and mixture alternately in a shallow 1-quart baking dish. Top with crumbs. Bake at 375° for 30 minutes or until bubbly. Makes 6 servings.

Stuffed Acorn Squash

2 acorn squash, cut in half
1 c. unsweetened applesauce
4 tsp. brown sugar
4 tsp. milk-free margarine
cinnamon

Place squash halves, cut side down, in shallow baking pan. Cover bottom with water. Bake at 400° for 50 to 60 minutes or until tender. Turn squash over. Fill each cavity with applesauce and brown sugar. Dot with milk-free margarine. Sprinkle with cinnamon. Continue baking until applesauce is bubbly, about 15 to 20 minutes. Makes 4 servings.

Oven Creamed Potatoes

4 c. raw, diced potatoes
4 tbsp. milk-free margarine
3 tbsp. flour
1/8 tsp. pepper
1½ c. milk substitute
1 tsp. salt

Put potatoes in greased baking dish. Melt "butter," add flour, and mix well. Gradually add milk and cook, stirring constantly until thickened. Add seasonings. Pour over potatoes, cover and bake at 350° for 1¼ hours. Uncover during last 15 minutes, if desired, to brown slightly.

Milk-Free
Egg-Free

Carrots Carolina

About 30 minutes before serving:

Start heating oven to 375°F. Thoroughly drain two 1-pound cans whole baby carrots. In a metal 8 x 8 x 2-inch square pan, mix together ½ cup firmly packed dark-brown sugar, 2 tablespoons orange or pineapple juice, and dash salt. Cook, stirring constantly, until sugar is dissolved. Add carrots: stir to coat with sugar mixture. Bake, stirring occasionally, for 20 minutes. Serve with syrup. Makes 6 servings.

Green Bean Casserole

> 1 lb. beans (green, cut)
> 2 med. green peppers seeded and chopped
> 4 med. white onions, chopped

Grease casserole. Place in alternate layers beginning and ending with green beans. Sprinkle with salt, paprika and milk-free margarine. Cover and bake at 350° for one hour. The last few minutes, uncover and top with milk-free bread crumbs.

Spicy Green Beans

> 1 pkg. (9 oz.) frozen French-style green beans
> ½ c. finely chopped celery
> ¼ c. finely chopped onion
> 2 tbsp. chopped pimento
> 1 tbsp. water
> ¼ tsp. dill weed
> 1 tbsp. vinegar
> ⅛ tsp. pepper

Cook green beans according to directions for panned vegetables (recipe follows). Add remaining ingredients. Toss lightly and heat (celery and onion will be crisp). Makes 4 servings.

Panned Vegetables

> 1 tbsp. milk-free margarine
> 1-2 tbsp. water
> 1 pkg. (9-10 oz.) frozen vegetables
> salt

Measure milk-free margarine, water and salt into saucepan. Add frozen vegetables. Cook over low heat, stirring often with a fork to separate vegetables. Cover and cook only until tender. Length of time will depend on variety of vegetable. More water may be added, but only as needed. Makes 3 to 4 servings.

Corn Pie*

The Coffee Rich way to make canned corn exciting—perfect with roast meat or steak.

> 1½ c. fine cracker crumbs
> ½ c. melted milk-free margarine
> 2 tbsp. milk-free margarine
> 1 c. Coffee Rich
> ½ tsp. onion salt
> ¼ c. Coffee Rich
> 2 c. corn, drained (#303 can)
> ¼ tsp. pepper
> 2 tbsp. flour

Preheat oven to 350°. Melt milk-free margarine and toss with crumbs. Reserve ½ cup of crumbs for top; use the remainder to line 9-inch pie shell. Put milk-free margarine, 1 cup Coffee Rich, corn, onion, salt and pepper in sauce pan. In small bowl, add ¼ cup Coffee Rich to flour: mix to a smooth paste. Blend into corn mixture. Cook until slightly thickened. Pour into cracker-lined pie shell, top with reserved ½ cup crumbs. Bake in 350° oven 45 minutes or until silver knife inserted in center comes out clean. Serve hot. Yield: 6 servings. Preparation time: 40 minutes.

---

*Reprinted with permission from Rich Products Corp., P.O. Box 245, 1145 Niagara St., Buffalo, N.Y.

Milk-Free
Egg-Free

Broccoli Coffee Rich*

An elegant, inexpensive vegetable entree

> 1 10-oz. pkg. frozen, chopped broccoli, cooked
> ¾ c. cooked noodles
> 1 tbsp. flour
> salt and pepper to taste
> 3 tbsp. pecans, broken into pieces
> 1 tbsp. milk-free margarine
> ¾ c. Coffee Rich

Preheat oven to 350°.
Cook broccoli and noodles or use leftovers. Melt milk-free margarine. Blend in flour and seasonings. Slowly add Coffee Rich. Cook with stirring until thickened. Combine sauce with broccoli and noodles: pour into buttered 1-quart casserole. Top with nuts and bake in 350° oven for 20 minutes or until heated through and bubbly.
Yield: 4 servings
Preparation time: 30 minutes

Note: Casserole can be prepared ahead of time and refrigerated, allowing a little longer for baking.

Don's Blender Hollandaise
(About 1 cup)

> ½ c. milk-free margarine (1 stick)
> 4 egg yolks
> 2 to 3 tbsp. freshly squeezed lemon juice
> dash of pepper
> ¼ tsp. salt

Heat milk-free margarine until bubbly. Meanwhile, place egg yolks, fresh lemon juice, salt and pepper in electric blender. Turn blender on and off quickly. Then turn to high speed and slowly

---

*Reprinted with permission from Rich Products Corp., P.O. Box 245, 1145 Niagara St., Buffalo, N.Y.

add bubbly milk-free margarine in a very thin, but steady, stream. Turn off blender and serve immediately over broccoli, asparagus, or grilled tomatoes. On fish. Or to make Eggs Benedict.

White Sauce*

1 tbsp. milk-free margarine
1 cup milk substitute
1 tbsp. wheat or potato flour
salt to taste

Melt milk-free margarine and add wheat or potato flour, stirring until blended. To margarine-flour mixture, slowly add the milk-substitute, stirring constantly until well-blended. If a thicker sauce is desired, increase margarine and flour to 2 tablespoons of each.

Barbecue Sauce

Sauté until transparent: 1 large onion, finely chopped, and 1 cup of oil. Add 1 teaspoon garlic salt, 1 cup chopped mushrooms (small can), and 1 tablespoon milk-free margarine. To season, add 1 teaspoon oregano, 1 teaspoon tarragon, and 1 dash of sage. Then add 1 tablespoon of sweet chili powder mixed with 3 small cans of tomato paste. Simmer gently for 30 minutes. Add salt and pepper to taste, $\frac{1}{2}$ cup chopped olives, $\frac{1}{2}$ cup chopped pickle relish with liquid, and $\frac{1}{2}$ cup chopped parsley. Use hot or cold on chops, roasts, hamburgers or hot dogs.

Sweet and Sour Sauce for Spareribs†

Chop and fry 1 onion and 1 green pepper.

1 c. (14 oz.) pineapple chunks
2 tsp. cornstarch
½ tsp. ground ginger
3 tbsp. vinegar

---

*Reprinted with permission from Allergy Information Association, Weston, Ontario, Canada.
†Reprinted with permission from Allergy Information Association, Weston, Ontario, Canada.

Drain pineapple juice into saucepan. Stir together a little syrup with cornstarch and pour into syrup in pan. Cook, stirring until thick and clear. Stir in vinegar and ginger. Add onions and peppers. Use to bake spareribs for 45 minutes.

Milk-Free
Egg-Free

Superb Baked Beans

*3 lb. glass jar American Beauty Old Fashioned Great Northern Beans® packed by Morgan Packing Co., Austin, Indiana (these are in water, use beans and water as is).
1 c. sugar (white) for each cup and ½ beans and liquid
2 sticks unsalted, milk-free margarine
salt and pepper to taste

Cut milk-free margarine into small pieces and mix all ingredients. Bake at 275° for 3-3½ hours until done, stirring occasionally. Use flat, uncovered pan or casserole. Spread about ½ to 1 inch thick. Beans are done when clear and shiny and fluid is absorbed. If not tender, add more water during cooking (½ cup at a time) and cook until tender and transparent. These beans never fail to be the highlight of the meal.

Easy Barley Casserole

Great for buffet supper, we love it

¼ lb. milk-free margarine
¾ lb. sliced mushrooms
3 pimentos, chopped
salt and pepper
2 med. onions chopped
1½ c. pearl barley
2 c. chicken stock

Melt margarine in saucepan. Saute onions and mushrooms until

---

*3 lb. pre-soaked beans—either soak them yourself overnight in water to cover or buy the above.

tender. Add barley and cook until brown, Add pimentos, chicken stock, and salt and pepper to taste. Cover and bake at 350° for 50-60 minutes. If dry, add more stock.

Foil Potatoes

Special!

For each person:

> 1 med. potato
> 1 tbsp. milk-free margarine
> 2 tbsp. prepared onion soup mix

Pare potato. Cut in $\frac{1}{4}$-inch slices. Place slices on a square of heavy duty foil. Dot with milk-free margarine. Sprinkle with soup mix. Wrap and seal tightly. Roast on outdoor grill or in a 375° oven for about 45 minutes or until potatoes are tender.

Peas Oriental

> 1 pkg. frozen peas
> ½ c. sliced water chestnuts
> 1 pkg. French dressing

Bake at 350° for one hour in aluminum foil. Yield: 4 servings.

Soups are another food item hard to find commercially without the inclusion of some blend of milk or milk derivative. The following may help to add variety to your menus.

Quick Hot Tomato Bouillon

> 1 lg. can seasoned tomato juice cocktail or V-8® juice
> 1 can beef bouillon (optional)
> 2-3 tbsp. sugar
> whole cloves
> 1 orange, peeled and sliced

Put all ingredients in a kettle and simmer at a low boil for 10 minutes. Serve hot, in mugs, using the slice of orange stuffed with 3-4 cloves as garnish (after it has simmered with the soup). May also be jelled for tomato aspic and garnished with mayonnaise.

Milk-Free
Egg-Free

Jellied Chicken Bouillon

Wonderful summer luncheon dish with a salad or sandwich.

> chopped parsley
> 2 cups boiling chicken soup
> 1 envelope unflavored gelatin
> salt
> ¼ cup cold water

Make chicken soup, season well. Soak gelatin in cold water 5 minutes. Add soup and stir until dissolved. When slightly cool, add parsley. Chill. Stir lightly with a fork and serve in bouillon cups.

Milk-Free
Egg-Free

Tomato Bisque*

½ c. dry milk-free bread crumbs or corn flakes
2 tbsp. milk-free margarine
1 28-oz. can tomatoes
½ onion, sliced
2 c. milk substitute
1 beef bouillon cube
salt to taste
1 bay leaf
1 teaspoon sugar
few grains pepper
¼ tsp. nutmeg, if desired

Combine tomatoes, onion and bay leaf. Simmer for 10 minutes and press through sieve. Slowly stir in milk substitute, add bouillon cube dissolved in small amount of hot mixture. Add seasonings. Stir while heating. Do *not* boil. Add crumbs and milk-free margarine.

Jellied Consommeé

Delicious

2 cans beef bouillon
1 can chicken bouillon
1 can (8 oz.) tomato puree
2 egg whites, beaten
2 crushed eggshells
1 onion
1 small bunch parsley
salt and pepper to taste
2 env. unflavored gelatin
½ c. cold water

*Reprinted with permission from Allergy Information Association, Weston, Ontario, Canada.

Boil first 8 ingredients for 10 minutes: add gelatin soaked in cold water, stir to dissolve. Let stand 5 minutes, strain. Pour into cups with a slice of hard-cooked egg in the bottom of cup. Chill until firm. Serve with slice of lemon on edge of cup or with catsup or horseradish.

Milk-Free
Egg-Free

Dried Pea Soup

For those who love pea soup

smoked brisket of beef, ham bone, bacon, tongue or dried beef
2 c. split peas
1 small onion, cut fine
2 tbsp. shortening
1 tsp. sugar
¼ tsp. pepper
3 qt. cold water
¼ c. celery, diced
2 tbsp. flour
2 tsp. salt

Pick over and wash the peas. Soak them in cold water overnight or for several hours: if quick-cooking peas are used, do not soak. Drain, place in soup kettle with smoked beef, ham bone, tongue or bacon, add the cold water. Cover. Boil slowly but steadily 4 hours or more (quick cooking peas require shorter cooking) . Add the celery and cook until the peas and meat are tender. Remove meat when tender and place on platter. Skim fat off the top of soup. Heat 2 tablespoons fat in skillet, add the onions and brown, add flour and gradually add a cup of the soup. Add to the rest of soup. Season to taste and serve with croutons. Or cook peas until tender, add sliced smoked sausage or dried beef, boil a few minutes, and serve hot in the soup. A slice of toasted rye (milk-free) bread may be boiled with the soup. If soup is too thick, thin with soup stock.

Milk-Free
Egg-Free

Quick Potato Bisque*

Easy, easy and uses ingredients you have on your pantry shelf

1 chicken bouillon cube
1 tsp. onion salt
1½ c. instant potato flakes
2 c. water
⅛ tsp. pepper
3 c. Coffee Rich

Combine bouillon cubes, water and seasonings in saucepan and bring to boil. Heat until bouillon cube is melted. Stir in potato flakes and Coffee Rich and heat through. Garnish with chopped parsley or chives.

Onion Soup

3 tbsp. milk-free margarine
3 lg. onions, thinly sliced
pepper
1 tbsp. flour
½ tsp. salt
5 c. beef broth
4-6 slices milk-free Italian or French bread

Melt the margarine. Add the onions and cook slowly until golden. Sprinkle on the flour and simmer slowly a couple of minutes. Add seasoning and broth and simmer for about 30 minutes. Toast the bread and butter with margarine. Then return to the toaster very briefly. Serve in individual bowls with a piece of the toasted bread floating on the top of each.

---

*Reprinted with permission from Rich Products Corp., P.O. Box 245, 1145 Niagara St., Buffalo, N.Y.

CHAPTER 10

SALADS

HERE IS A HAPPY item for those on milk-free diets. With the exception of Roquefort or bleu cheese and caesar dressings, many salad variations need no special recipes. Follow any good cookbook. Greens, fruits, gelatin varieties as well as heartier salads with meats (watch cold cuts for milk, but use ham, milk-free bologna, etc.) can all be enjoyed. Some croutons are on the market in milk-free form, for example, onion-rye or those made from milk-free bread. If not available, use the recipe in this chapter for salad croutons. Remember, serve plenty of salads to your milk-free dieter.

Milk-Free Salad Croutons

Cut milk-free bread (rye is very good) into squares. Dry on cookie sheet in 200° oven about one-half hour or until dry and crisp. Sprinkle with your favorite spices, such as onion salt or powder, lemon-dill, paprika, or garlic salt or powder. Package in plastic bags or air tight jars for use on salads, casseroles and soups.

Bean Sprout and Spinach Salad

Drain and soak in cold water for several hours in refrigerator, 1 cup canned bean sprouts. Wash and refrigerate ½ pound spinach leaves.

In a bowl:

¼ c. soy sauce
2 tbsp. grated onion
½ tsp. pepper
½ c. oil
1½ tbsp. grated onion
½ tsp. sugar

Prepare dressing 1 hour before using to blend well. Put spinach in salad bowl. Top with bean sprouts, add ½ cup of water chestnuts, pour dressing, toss.

Confetti Coleslaw

3 c. shredded cabbage
½ c. green pepper strips
½ c. shredded carrot
2/3 c. cole slaw dressing

Place cabbage, carrot and green pepper in mixing bowl. Mix well. Add dressing and toss lightly. Makes 6 servings.

Potato Salad

2½ lb. potatoes
3 tbsp. white vinegar
1 tbsp. prepared mustard
¼ tsp. pepper
1 jar, (14 oz.) pimentos, whole pods, drained, cut into large pieces
3 tbsp. bacon chips
½ c. salad oil
3 tbsp. chopped onion
1 tsp. salt
½ tsp. celery seed
lettuce

Wash potatoes. Heat 1-inch salted water (½ teaspoon salt to 1 cup water) to boiling. Add unpared potatoes. Cover tightly: heat to boiling and cook 30 to 35 minutes or until tender. Drain: cool and peel. Cut potatoes into slices. Combine oil, vinegar, onion, mustard, salt and pepper: pour over potatoes and toss gently with pimentos. Cover: refrigerate at least 2 hours. Just before serving, add bacon chips and celery seeds: toss until potatoes are well-coated. Spoon into lettuce-lined salad bowl. If desired, garnish with bacon chips and pimentos. Makes 6-8 servings.

Party Potato Salad

Firmly pack 2 quarts of your favorite milk-free potato salad into a 9 × 5 × 3-inch loaf pan. Chill at least 2 hours. Unmold and glaze following this recipe:

> 1 envelope unflavored gelatin
> ½ c. cold chicken broth
> 1 c. milk-free mayonnaise

Sprinkle gelatin over broth in small saucepan: soften. Dissolve over low heat. Remove and stir in milk-free mayonnaise. Let stand 10 minutes. Spoon half of glaze over loaf to coat top and sides. Let stand 10 minutes. Spoon on remaining glaze to coat evenly. Immediately garnish as desired. Chill until ready to serve. Makes 12 (⅔ cup) servings.

Cling Peach Souffle Salad

Dissolve one package lime Jell-O in one cup of hot water. Add ½ cup of cold water, one tablespoon vinegar, ½ cup milk-free mayonnaise, and ¼ teaspoon salt. Blend with rotary beater and pour into refrigerator freezing tray.

Quick chill from 15 to 20 minutes, or until mixture is firm, about one inch from the edge, but soft to touch in the center. Turn into a bowl and whip with rotary beater until fluffy and creamy smooth. Fold in ½ cup diced celery, 3 tablespoons sweet pickle relish, 1½ cups canned peaches drained and cut up. Pour into one quart mold. Chill until firm in refrigerator (not freezing unit) for 30-60 minutes. Unmold, cut into servings. May garnish with peaches and mayonnaise or topping.

Waldorf Salad

> 1 can (13½ ounces) pineapple chunks, well-drained
> 2½ c. chopped tart apples
> ¼ c. chopped celery
> chopped walnut
> ½ c. mayonnaise (milk-free)

Place pineapple, apples and celery in mixing bowl. Toss lightly with dressing. Sprinkle with chopped walnuts. Makes 6 servings.

Milk-Free
Egg-Free

Eggless Mayonnaise or Salad Dressing

½ tsp. salt
3 tbsp. Coffee Rich
¼ tsp. paprika
½ c. salad oil
¼ tsp. dry mustard
¼ tbsp. lemon juice
few grains pepper
fresh cake of soy cheese (Tofu®)

Mix ingredients. Put in blender and beat until smooth and thick.

Soy Cheese Salad Dressing

2 heaping tbsp. mayonnaise
2 tbsp. Coffee Rich
3 heaping tbsp. chopped, canned soy cheese (soy bean curd or Tofu®)
3 heaping tbsp. salad oil
pepper
1 tbsp. white wine vinegar
cruhed clove garlic or ½ tbsp. garlic salt

Thin down mayonnaise with Coffee Rich. Add soy cheese and blend well. Stir in oil, vinegar and pepper and stir until all are well-blended (put the clove of garlic in oil for flavor, but be sure to remove the clove before pouring over salad) .

Milk-Free
Egg-Free

Macaroni or Potato Dressing*

3 tbsp. flour
1 tsp. salt
¾ c. Rich's Coffee Rich
¼ c. vinegar
3 tbsp. sugar
1 tsp. thyme
¾ c. water

Mix dry ingredients in pan. Add Coffee Rich and water gradually and stir until thick. Add vinegar and mix well.

Spinach Salad

2 c. raw spinach leaves, washed, broken into pieces without stems
    and drained
½ small can pimentos, chopped
⅛-¼ c. bacon bits
½ c. croutons

Mix with oil and vinegar or Italian or herb dressing to which 1 teaspoon of sugar has been added for each ½ cup of dressing. Variations: add hard-boiled eggs, tomato wedges, marinated mushrooms.

Apple Sauce De Luxe

canned apple sauce
sugar
Rich's topping
orange juice
lady fingers

Blend canned applesauce with orange juice and sugar to taste. Spoon into goblets or dessert dishes and insert a few lady fingers along the side. Top with Rich's whipped topping or Rich Whip.

*Reprinted with permission from Allergy Information Association, Weston, Ontario, Canada.

Citrus Maraschino Mold

3 env. plain gelatin
¾ c. strained orange juice
20 red maraschino cherries, quartered, or another canned fruit
1 can (11 oz.) mandarin oranges, drained
½ c. small seedless grapes (white) or ½ c. seeded malaga grapes
1/3 c. sugar
1/3 c. lemon juice
¼ c. lime juice
½ c. cold water
1/3 c. graefruit juice
1/3 c. orange juice
additional cherries and grapes

Soften 1 envelope of the gelatin in cold water. Add strained orange juice and stir over low heat until gelatin is dissolved. Cool. Pour half into a square pan. Chill until set. Reserve remaining orange gelatin at room temperature. Lightly mark gelatin layer into quarters with toothpick. Arrange cherries in two opposite quarters, mandarin oranges in third and grapes in fourth. Carefully pour remaining orange gelatin over fruit and chill until set. Meanwhile combine remaining gelatin with sugar and fruit juices. Stir over low heat until gelatin is dissolved. Chill until nearly set. Turn into mixing bowl and beat with electric beater until tripled in volume and very pale in color. Spoon into mold and chill for at least 2 hours. To serve, unmold and garnish with whole cherries and grapes.

Easy Tomato Aspic

1 14-oz. can tomato juice
1 tsp. Worcestershire sauce
1 pkg. lemon gelatin
1 tbsp. vinegar

Use any or all of the following ingredients as desired or use shrimp, crabmeat, chicken, ham etc. Use in all 2 cups.

1 c. chopped celery
3 tbsp. chopped green peppers
3 tbsp. chopped carrots
1 tbsp. grated onion
3 tbsp. chopped pickles or pickle relish
3 tbsp. chopped cucumbers
3 tbsp. chopped, stuffed olives
1 tsp. sliced radishes
½ c. canned, drained mushrooms

Bring tomato juice to boil. Dissolve in it the package of gelatin. Add vinegar and chopped foods. Pour into a medium-sized, greased mold and refrigerate. May be made in a square pan and cut into squares. Serve with mayonnaise, cottage cheese, or mild horseradish sauce.

Ginger Ale Fruit Salad

2 tbsp. gelatin
½ c. boiling orange juice or any fruit juice
½ c. sugar
1 pt. ginger ale
½ lb. white grapes, washed, stemmed
1 sliced orange, skinned
1 small can pineapple chunks
4 tbsp. cold water
⅛ tsp. salt
juice of 1 lemon
1 sliced grapefruit, skinned and sectioned

Add cold water to gelatin. Add gelatin to fruit juice and dissolve. Then add sugar, salt, ginger ale, and lemon juice. Chill to jelly consistency, then add grapes, orange, grapefruit and pineapple chunks. Pour in wet mold and chill till firm or chill in individual molds. Serve on lettuce. Garnish as desired. Will make 8-10 servings.

Special Chicken or Turkey Salad

 2 c. diced cooked chicken or turkey
 1/2 c. diced fine green pepper
 1/2 c. sliced celery
 1 c. green grapes
 1/2 c. sliced spanish olives (optional)
 2 tsp. capers (optional)
 1 can Mandarin orange sections drained

Combine all ingredients and mix with mayonnaise. Serve on lettuce and sprinkle with paprika. Decorate with deviled eggs, sliced hard-cooked eggs, or tomato wedges as desired.

CHAPTER 11
SANDWICHES AND CANAPÉS

THE SCHOOL CHILD who is a milk-free dieter must, of necessity, take his or her lunch to school for his entire school career. (This cookbook was a collection of recipes until my son went to college and lived in a fraternity, then I organized the recipes for the cook there and the cookbook took form.) Because of the lunch problem I added a list of sandwiches as suggestions for the lunch pail. Along with sandwiches I added raw vegetables—celery, carrots, peppers etc.—raisins in small boxes, and oatmeal or molasses cookies. Sometimes a salad was included. Variety always helped and often a small jar of Jell-O or a fruit prepared for eating was added. Fruits raw were not well-eaten because of the time factor, but 1 would peel or slice an orange or apple and re-assemble it in the lunch or add grapes or fruit cocktail.

Sandwiches with Milk-Free Bread

Tuna fish
Bacon or bacon, lettuce and tomato
Club sandwich
Milk-free bologna or cold cuts
Ham
Ground ham (see Ground Ham Sandwich Spread)
Chicken
Chicken salad
Chicken spread (see Canapés)
Peanut butter
Peanut butter and jelly
Roast beef or leftover roasted meat such as lamb, veal,
    beef, chicken or pork
Corned beef
Hot dogs (look for kosher varieties or all-beef, milk-free)
Egg sandwiches

Ground Ham Sandwich Spread

Grind cooked ham in grinder. Mix with mayonnaise, a little prepared mustard, and a little sharp mustard. Mix until right consistency to spread. Stores well in covered jar in refrigerator for several days.

VARIATIONS:
1. May add a little pickle relish or ripe olives.
2. Use on crackers for canapés: decorate with green peppers or parsley.

Canapés

*Raw Vegetables and Dips**

> carrots
> cauliflower
> celery
> cucumbers
> radishes
> green onions
> cherry tomatoes
> green peppers

Arrange washed and trimmed vegetables on a tray. Serve with a variety of dunking sauces.

Horseradish Sauce†

> 2 tbsp. horseradish
> 1 tsp. meat sauce
> 2 tsp. Worcestershire sauce
> ½ c. chili sauce
> 1/3 c. mayonnaise

Mix all ingredients well. Store in jar in refrigerator.

---

*Reprinted with permission from Allergy Information Association, Weston, Ontario, Canada.
†Reprinted with permission from Allergy Information Association, Weston, Ontario, Canada.

Dill Dip‡

4 egg yolks
5 tsp. prepared mustard
1 tsp. salt
2 tbsp. dried dill
½ tsp. pepper
1 tbsp. sugar
1 c. salad oil
2 tbsp. vinegar

Beat egg yolks. Add next 5 ingredients and beat well. Add oil, one teaspoon at a time, beating constantly. Add vinegar and beat.

Curry Dip*

½ c. mayonnaise
½ c. non-dairy frozen creamer
1 tsp. curry powder
½ tsp. lemon juice

Mix all ingredients well. Chill. Keep in refrigerator.

Chicken Spread

Grind cooked chicken. Mix with mayonnaise. Season and spread on bread rounds or crackers. Decorate with pimentoes or parsley.

Onion Soup Dip

For potato chips, corn chips etc. Mix mayonnaise with non-fat frozen creamer until consistency of boiled custard. Mix with an envelope of dried onion soup.

---

‡Reprinted with permission from Allergy Information Association, Weston, Ontario, Canada.
*Reprinted with permission from Allergy Information Association, Weston, Ontario, Canada.

Dill Dip

Same as above using prepared dill mixture for dips.

Bacon Dip

Use bacon chips or bits of dried chipped beef.

Small Hot Dogs or Sausages

Tiny, milk-free hot dogs or sausages, grilled. Thread on tooth-picks while hot, with chunks of grilled pineapple.

Cocktail Meatballs—I

2 lb. ground chuck
¼ c. milk-free bread crumbs or corn flakes
2 14-oz. bottles pizza-flavored catsup
1 10-oz. jar currant or apple jelly
1 env. onion soup mix
2 teaspoons monsodium glutamate
2 tablespoons milk-free margarine
1 egg (omit for egg-free)

Early on day of serving: In large bowl, mix together ground chuck, onion soup mix, egg, monsodium glutamate, and milk-free bread crumbs. With hands, form into bite-size meatballs. Arrange on cookie sheet: cover with Saran Wrap,® refrigerate (or in skillet, in hot milk-free margarine, sauté meatballs until brown all over. Remove from skillet, cool, wrap in plastic wrap and re-frigerate.) In electric skillet, set at 215° or in large skillet over medium heat, stir together catsup and jelly until blended. Add meatballs: simmer, covered about 25 minutes or until heated through. Serve in electric skillet set at warm, or in chafing dish over candle, to keep meatballs and sauce hot. Let guests pick up the meatballs with toothpicks. Makes about four dozen meatballs.

Cocktail Meat Balls*—II

An oh-so-easy cocktail tidbit

> 1 lb. lean ground beef
> 1/3 cup dry (milk-free) bread crumbs
> 1 egg
> 1 tbsp. sweet pickle relish
> 2 tbsp. oil
> 2 tbsp. cornstarch
> ½ tsp. salt
> 1/3 cup red wine
> 1 tbsp. grated onion
> ½ tsp. garlic salt
> 1 cup Coffee Rich
> ½ cup red wine
> 2 tsp. Worcestershire sauce

Preheat oven to 400°. Mix ground beef, bread crumbs, wine, eggs and seasonings. Form into 24 walnut-sized meatballs. Place in baking dish. Brush meat balls with oil. Bake in 400° oven for 20 minutes. Pour off excess fat. Combine Coffee Rich, wine, cornstarch, salt and Worcestershire sauce and pour over meat balls. Return to 400° oven and bake 10 minutes longer. Yield: 24 cocktail meat balls. Preparation time: 30 minutes.

Note: If desired, meat balls can be made in skillet on top of range.

---

*Reprinted with permission from Rich Products Corp., P.O. Box 245, 1145 Niagara St., Buffalo, N.Y.

CHAPTER 12

DESSERTS

Blueberry Dessert

1 c. sifted cake flour
$\frac{1}{2}$ c. + 2 tbsp. sugar
3 tbsp. soft shortening
$\frac{1}{2}$ tsp. vanilla
3 egg whites
$\frac{3}{4}$ c. sugar
1 cup fresh blueberries, or to taste with blueberry pie filling
$1\frac{1}{2}$ tsp. baking powder
$\frac{1}{4}$ tsp. salt
$\frac{1}{2}$ c. milk substitute
3 egg yolks
$\frac{1}{4}$ tsp. cream of tartar
$\frac{1}{2}$ tsp. vanilla

Grease and flour one 9-inch round cake pan. Sift together flour, sugar, baking powder, and salt. Add shortening. Pour in a little over half the milk substitute and $\frac{1}{2}$ teaspoon vanilla. Beat 2 minutes. Add remaining milk substitute and egg yolks and beat 2 minutes. Pour into prepared pan but do not bake yet. Make a meringue by beating together until foamy the egg whites and cream of tartar. Gradually beat in the sugar and vanilla. Pile lightly over batter, evenly in center, but mounding around the edges of the cake so as to form a basket effect. Bake at 350° for 35-40 minutes or until brown and done. Cool 20 minutes in pan, then loosen sides with a knife and invert on a folded towel on palm of hand and place right side up on wire rack to finish cooling. Add blueberries just before serving.

Fruit Juice Snow

1 env. unflavored gelatin
1 can frozen concentrate fruit juice (orange, lemon, Hawaiian Punch®,
   pineapple-orange, etc.)
½ c. sugar
½ c. water and ¾ c. water
⅛ tsp. salt

Melt gelatin, sugar and salt. Add ½ cup water. Place on low heat
until dissolved. Remove from heat, stir in remaining ¾ cup water
and frozen juice. Stir until melted. Chill. Add two or three unbeaten egg whites and beat in electric beater until mixture begins
to hold its shape. Spoon into dessert dishes.

Banana Freeze

½ c. sugar
1 tbsp. lemon juice (fresh, frozen or canned)
1 egg white
1 lg. ripe banana
¾ c. orange juice (fresh, frozen or canned)
1 c. water
2/3 c. water

Cook sugar and water together until sugar dissolves. Remove from
heat and stir in salt, mashed or sieved banana, orange juice, and
lemon juice. Pour mixture into two refrigerator trays and freeze
until mixture is mushy. This usually takes about 1 hour. Beat
egg white and water until stiff. Mix thoroughly, but gently, into
the partially frozen mixture. Return to trays. Freeze until firm.
Yield: about 10 servings.

Lady Finger Dessert

2 boxes German semi-sweet chocolate
4 tbsp. water
4 eggs, separated and beaten well
vanilla
2 tbsp. sugar
1 pkg. Lady Fingers

Beat egg whites till stiff, gradually add sugar and beat again. Melt chocolate and water. Add slowly to well-beaten egg yolk and vanilla mixture. Fold chocolate mixture into egg whites. Line a dish with $\frac{1}{2}$ Lady Fingers, sides vertically and flat on bottom. Pour mixture over the lady fingers and fill bowl. Refrigerate to set and serve cold.

Lemon Snow*

1 c. sugar
2½ tsp. powdered gelatin
1 grated lemon rind
juice from 2 lemons
5 eggs

Dissolve gelatin in warm water. Combine egg yolks with sugar and beat until creamy and light. To this mixture add the lemon juice and grated lemon rind. Beat egg whites until stiff. Add by folding into lemon juice mixture. Add in the dissolved gelatin, stirring slowly. Pour mixture into glass or a serving bowl. Chill until time to serve. Yield: 6 servings.

Gingerbread

A lighter gingerbread than Gingerbread II

1/3 c. vegetable shortening or milk-free margarine
1 c. sugar
1 tsp. salt
3 tsp. baking powder
1½ c. milk-substitute
1 egg
2 c. flour less 2 tbsp.
1 tsp. ginger

Blend the milk-free margarine and sugar: add the egg, well-beaten. Add the dry ingredients alternately with milk substitute.

---

*Reprinted with permission from Allergy Information Association, Weston, Ontario, Canada.

Mix again. Spread thin on greased 9 × 13-inch pan. Bake 15 minutes in a 350° oven. Sprinkle with sugar, cut in squares before removing from pan.

Gingerbread II with Caramel Sauce*

      1 c. molasses
      1 tsp. cinnamon
      ¼ tsp. nutmeg
      ½ c. milk-free margarine
      1 c. boiling water
      2 tsp. baking soda
      1 tsp. ginger
      ½ c. sugar
      2 c. flour (scant)
      2 eggs, beaten separately

Mix molasses, soda and spices. Add sugar, butter, flour and water: beat well. Add egg yolks and fold in whites. Pour in a greased (8-cup) ring mold and bake in a 350° oven 35-40 minutes. (Don't worry if batter seems thin: it's supposed to be.)

Caramel Sauce

      2 egg yolks
      1 lb. light brown sugar (2¼ c)
      1 tbsp. milk-free margarine
      1 tsp. vanilla
      1 c. milk substitute
      ⅛ tsp. salt

Add egg yolks and milk substitute to sugar. Cook until creamy in double boiler. Add milk-free margarine. When cool, add vanilla and salt. Serve gingerbread on a large, round platter. Both are even nicer when served warm. Serves 8.

---

*Everyone loves this version.

English Cake Dessert

1 c. powdered sugar, sifted
2/3 c. cornstarch, sifted
1/8 tsp. cream of tartar
1/2 tsp. vanilla
3 eggs, separated
2 tsp. water

Sift ½ cup sugar and cornstarch 3 times. Beat egg whites, water, and cream of tartar to soft peaks. Beat in ½ cup sugar a little at a time until stiff peaks form. Beat yolks and vanilla until blended and add to whites. Fold in the sugar and cornstarch gradually. Bake in two 8-inch layer tins in 350° oven about 30 minutes. Put layers together with drained fruits, bananas, boiled custard or other desired filling. (May be frozen).

Fluffy Frosting

2 egg whites
1 tsp. lemon juice
2 tsp. cornstarch
1 tbsp. vinegar
pinch of salt
2½ c. icing sugar (confectioner's)

Beat egg whites until stiff but not dry. Add vinegar, lemon juice, salt and cornstarch. Continue beating. Gradually add icing sugar until mixture can be spread. Frost cake, heaping high in center of cake. Decorate as desired.

---

*Reprinted with permission from Allergy Information Association, Weston, Ontario, Canada.

Milk-Free
Egg-Free

Marshmallow Treats*

¼ c. milk-free margarine
7-10 ozs. regular marshmallows (about 40)
        or 3 cups miniature marshmallows (milk-free)
5-6 c. Rice Krispies®

Melt butter in 3-quart saucepan. Add marshmallows and cook over low heat, stirring constantly, until marshmallows are melted and mixture is well-blended. Remove from heat. Add Rice Krispies and stir until well-coated. Press warm mixture into buttered 13 × 9-inch pan. Cut into squares when cool. Yield: 24 (2-inch) squares.

VARIATIONS:

Marshmallow Crispy Dream Bars

Press warm marshmallow crispy mixture into buttered 13 × 9 inch pan. Cut into 2 × 1-inch bars. Dip ends of bars into melted semisweet chocolate, then in chopped nutmeats. Place on waxed paper or buttered baking sheets to harden. Yield: 48 bars.

Chocolate Crispy Slices

Shape warm marshmallow crispy mixture into two rolls about 1½ inches in diameter. Let stand until hardened. Coat with melted semisweet chocolate. Cool and cut into slices.

Milk-Free
Egg-Free

Peach Betty with Lemon Sauce

About 1½ hours before serving: Start heating oven to 350°.

*Reprinted with permission from Allergy Information Association, Weston, Ontario, Canada.

Pour one 1-pound, 4-ounce can cling-peach slices and syrup into a 2-quart casserole: sprinkle with 2 tablespoons lemon juice and ½ teaspoon cinnamon. In a medium bowl, mix 1½ cups coarsely ground uncooked rolled oats, ½ teaspoon salt, ¼ teaspoon baking soda, and ⅓ cup firmly packed dark-brown sugar: stir in ¼ cup melted hydrogenated shortening and ½ teaspoon vanilla extract. Cover peaches with crumb mixture: bake 50 minutes. Serve with Lemon Sauce (below). Makes 6 servings.

Lemon Sauce

In a medium saucepan, mix together 3 tablespoons granulated sugar, 2 tablespoons cornstarch, ¼ teaspoon salt, and 1 teaspoon grated lemon peel. Slowly stir in 1 cup boiling water: cook, stirring constantly for 5 minutes. Stir in 2 tablespoons hydrogenated shortening and 2 tablespoons lemon juice. Serve over Peach Betty (above).

Bread Pudding

2 eggs
½ c. sugar
4 c. milk-free dry bread or cake in cubes
¼ c. raisins
2 c. milk substitute
nutmeg or cinnamon
almonds

Beat the eggs. Add milk substitute, sugar and gratings of nutmeg or cinnamon if desired: pour liquid over the bread in a pudding dish, let stand until thoroughly soaked. Add raisins and almonds, if desired. Bake 20 minutes or until firm in a moderate oven, 350°. Serve with topping, jelly, or any pudding sauce.

Milk-Free
Egg-Free

Old-Fashioned Rice Pudding

½ c. rice
½ teaspoon salt
½ c. sugar
4 c. milk substitute

Mix ingredients. Bake 2 hours in a buttered baking dish, covered, at 325°, until the rice has softened: uncover, brown slightly. Serve with milk and sugar.

Raisin Rice Pudding

2 c. cooked rice
⅛ tsp. salt
1 tbsp. milk-free margarine
2 eggs, well-beaten
¼ c. raisins
2 c. milk substitute
1/3 c. sugar
rind of ½ lemon, grated

Mix ingredients well. Bake 20 minutes in a moderate oven, 350°, in buttered baking dish, with bread crumbs at the top and bottom. If desired, fruit may be added to the rice in layers.

Milk-Free
Egg-Free

Rice Whip*

1½ c. cooked rice
⅛ tsp. salt
1 pkg. frozen strawberries
¼ c. sugar
¾ c. Rich Whip®

*Reprinted with permission from Allergy Information Association, Weston, Ontario, Canada.

Whip cream, add sugar and salt, and fold into cooked rice. Serve strawberries as sauce: over and under the rice whip is suggested. Yield: 4 servings.

VARIATIONS: Any other frozen fruit, chocolate sauce made with cocoa, or maple syrup may be used.

Tapioca Cream

1/3 c. quick-cooking tapioca
2 c. milk substitute
¼ tsp. salt
1 tsp. vanilla
2 eggs, separated
1/3 c. sugar

Add tapioca to the milk and cook in double boiler until the tapioca is clear. Beat the yolks, add the salt, sugar and the hot milk mixture, and cook until it thickens. Remove from the heat, cool, fold in the whites, beaten stiff. Flavor when cold. Or make meringue from egg whites and brown in oven a few minutes.

Meringue Shell*

3 egg whites
dash salt
¼ tsp. cream of tartar
1 tsp. vanilla
1 c. sugar

Have egg whites at room temperature. Add vanilla, cream of tartar, and salt. Beat until frothy. Gradually add sugar, a small amount at a time, beating till very stiff peaks and sugar is dissolved. Cover cookie sheets with plain ungreased paper. Using a 9-inch round cake pan as a guide, draw a circle on paper. Spread

*Reprinted with permission from Allergy Information Association, Weston, Ontario, Canada.

meringue over circle, shape into shell with back of spoon, making bottom ½ inch thick and mounding around edge to make sides 1¾ inches high. Bake in very slow oven (275°) for 1 hour. Turn off heat and let dry in oven (door closed) at least two hours. Fill as desired.

FOR INDIVIDUAL MERINGUE SHELLS: Draw eight 3⅓ inch circles, spread each with about ⅓ cup meringue. Shape with spoon to make shells. Bake as above.

Skillet Peach Dumplings*

Top of the range or electric skillet quick dessert

1 #2½ can sliced peaches
2 tbsp. milk-free margarine
2 tsp. baking powder
2 tbsp. milk-free margarine
½ c. Coffee Rich
½ tsp. grated lemon rind
cinnamon sugar
1¼ c. all-purpose flour
½ tsp. salt
1 egg
¼ tsp. almond flavoring

In skillet, bring to boil peaches, syrup and butter (milk-free margarine). Place in mixing bowl. Cut milk-free margarine into dry ingredients. Beat Coffee Rich, egg, and flavorings together. and add to dry ingredients. Drop by tablespoons into boiling fruit. Lower heat and cook dumplings uncovered for 10 minutes. Sprinkle with cinnamon sugar. Cover skillet and cook another 10 minutes over low heat. Serve hot with Rich Whip or Coffee Rich. Yield: 6 servings. Preparation Time: 30 minutes.

---

*Reprinted with permission from Rich Products Corp., 1145 Niagara St., Buffalo, N.Y.

Milk-Free
Egg-Free

Fruit Crisp Dessert*

1 can (16 oz.) peach halves
1 tsp. lemon juice
3 tbsp. brown sugar
½ tsp. salt
1 can (16 oz.) pear halves
2 c. rice cereal
1 tsp. grated lemon rind
3 tbsp. milk-free margarine

Remove fruit from juice and place halves, alternating peach and pear, hollow down in shallow 9-inch baking dish or pie plate. Add lemon juice to ¼ cup peach juice and ¼ cup pear juice; pour over fruit. Crush rice cereal into coarse crumbs. Mix with brown sugar, lemon rind, nutmeg and salt. Melt margarine, pour over crumb mixture, mix well. Spoon evenly over fruit. Bake at 350° for about 1 hour. Serve warm.

Milk-Free
Egg-Free

Apple Strudel†

3½ c. corn flakes, slightly crushed
2 c. sliced apples, sprinkled with few drops lemon juice
½ c. granulated sugar
2 tbsp. milk-free margarine
½ tsp. cinnamon or nutmeg

Butter baking dish. Arrange crumbs and apples in layers, sprinkle the apples with sugar and spices, and dot with margarine. Cover and bake at 375° for about 40 minutes or until apples are soft.

---

*Reprinted with permission from Allergy Information Association, Weston, Ontario, Canada.

†Reprinted with permission from Allergy Information Association, Weston, Ontario, Canada.

Apple Crunch

Very good—use half the amount for a square pan size.

1 c. sifted flour
1 tsp. cinnamon
½ c. vegetable margarine
¾ tsp. salt
½ c. brown sugar
5-6 med. cooking apples
½ c. coarsely chopped walnuts (optional)

Into a medium mixing bowl sift together the flour, salt, cinnamon and sugar. With a pastry blender thoroughly cut in milk-free margarine until mixture looks like crumbs. Peel, core and cut apples in eighths: slice crosswise thinly to make 6 cups. Turn apples into a rectangular baking pan (11 × 7 × 1½ inches), sprinkle with walnuts, and pile flour mixture on top (pan will be full, but apples sink during baking). Bake in a preheated 350° oven until apples are tender—about 55 minutes. Test apples by piercing with a fork. Place under broiler to brown top lightly. Serve warm plain or use a milk-free topping.

CHAPTER 13

PIES

Pies are easier desserts to find in the milk-free categories than most other varieties. Milk-free pie crust is not always found in boughten pies so, again, read the ingredients before buying a frozen or bakery-made pie or before buying pie crust mix.

Milk-Free Pie Crust

vegetable shortening or lard
ice water

Easily made milk-free. Simply use vegetable shortening or lard and ice water to make the crust. Use no butter or milk in the filling. *Follow any good cookbook's pie crust recipe.*

Pie Crust Dough

1½ c. flour
1 tsp. baking powder
¼ c. ice water
¼ tsp. salt
6 tbsp. milk-free margarine

Sift flour, salt, and baking powder together. Add milk-free margarine. Cut the shortening into the flour mixture using two knives until its largest bits are the size of a small pea. Sprinkle ice water over mixture and mix lightly to make a light dough. Handle only until it will hold together. Then chill 10 minutes before rolling. Makes 2 crusts.

Graham Cracker Crust

milk-free graham cracker crumbs
milk-free margarine

Follow the directions in any cookbook using milk-free graham
cracker crumbs and milk-free margarine to replace butter.

Fruit Pies

milk-free pie crust dough
fruit pie filling

Easily made using milk-free pie crust dough. For filling follow
any fruit pie filling, substituting milk-free margarine for butter.

Cream Pies

cornstarch
non-dairy frozen creamer

Not recommended, does not adapt well to substitution, but you
can try using cornstarch for thickening, non-dairy frozen creamer
for milk, and milk-free margarine for butter.

Berry Pies

Strawberry, blackberry, raspberry, blueberry, etc.

pie crust for top and bottom
2/3-1 c. sugar (more if needed)
4 tbsp. flour
1½ tbsp. lemon juice or ½ tsp. cinnamon
1 tbsp. milk-free margarine
4 c. fresh or frozen berries
2 tsp. tapioca

Prepare pie crust. Pick berries over and boil. Combine sugar, flour, tapioca, and lemon juice or cinnamon. Sprinkle over berries and mix gently. Put berries in lower crust and dot with milk-free margarine. Cover with upper crust or with lattice top. Bake in preheated 350° oven for 40-45 minutes until brown and bubbly. Be sure to put a sheet of foil below the pie to catch the juice.

Apple Pie

1 tbsp. flour
½ tsp. nutmeg
¾ c. orange juice
3 medium-sized, very tart apples, finely chopped
4 tbsp. melted milk-free margarine
1 c. sugar (some brown)
Unbaked pie crust (milk-free)

Stir flour into melted milk-free margarine. To this add nutmeg, orange juice, and sugar and mix together. Place chopped apples in pastry shell and pour above ingredients over them. Put strips of pastry over top and bake for 15 minutes in 450° oven. Reduce heat to 300° and bake until done—usually 25-30 minutes. Use a well-greased, 9-inch pie pan and your own favorite pastry recipe. Refrigerate 2 hours.

Strawberry Pie

1 qt. fresh strawberries, sliced
1 c. sugar
3 tbsp. cornstarch
1 c. water
1/3 c. water
cooked pie crust (milk-free)

Combine 1 cup strawberries, 1 cup sugar, and 1 cup water. Thicken with 3 tablespoons cornstarch and ⅓ cup water. Cool. Fill crust with remaining berries and cover with the glaze. May add topping if desired.

Lemon Pie

1 c. sugar
grated rind of 1 lemon
1½ c. warm water
1 tbsp. milk-free margarine
4 tbsp. cornstarch
juice of 2 lemons
3 egg yolks

Cook all in double boiler, stir until thick. Add 1 tablespoon milk-free margarine. Pour into baked pie shell and cover with a well-beaten meringue made from the 3 egg whites, ¾ cup sugar, ¼ teaspoon cream of tartar, and dash of salt. Cover the pie with the meringue and bake at 300° until meringue begins to brown.

Pecan Pie

3 tbsp. milk-free margarine
½ c. flour
3 eggs, slightly beaten
1/3 c. brown sugar
3 c. Karo® syrup
1 c. pecans
baked pie shell (milk-free)

Bake at 350° for 70 minutes.

Angel Pie

1 baked meringue shell (recipe follows)
filling (filling recipes follow)

Baked Meringue Shell

4 egg whites (½ c.) at room temperature
⅛ tsp. salt
1 c. very fine sugar
¼ tsp. cream of tartar

Preheat oven to 200°. Lightly grease and flour baking sheet, using 8-inch layer pans as a guide, mark 2 circles, *at least* 1 inch apart. Beat egg whites with salt and cream of tartar until just stiff but not dry. Gradually beat in sugar very slowly, and continue beating until no grains of sugar are felt when mixture is rubbed between fingers. Pile meringue mixture on two circles, pile edges and hollow out the middle like a deep pie crust. Bake 30 minutes at 225°. Turn off heat and keep in oven until dry and crisp. Cool. Then fill with your favorite filling and serve.

(Note: Do not make on a wet day.)

Fillings

Strawberry Angel Pie

1 pt. strawberries
1/16 tsp. salt
2 tbsp. lemon juice
1 c. granulated sugar
2 c. Rich Whip, whipped
2 egg whites, whipped

Wash and stem berries. Add sugar and crush. Heat until sugar is dissolved. Add salt, strain and chill. Add lemon juice to berry mixture. Fold in Rich Whip and stiffly beaten egg white to which salt has been added. Freeze in a tray.

Lemon Pie Filling (use prepared, milk-free)

Chocolate Filling

> 2 six oz. (2 c.) packages semisweet chocolate morsels
> ¼ c. light corn syrup
> ¼ c. water
> 1 c. Rich Whip, whipped
> 1 tbsp. instant coffee
> 3 egg yolks
> 1 tbsp. vanilla

Melt semisweet chocolate over hot (not boiling) water. Remove from hot water. Combine corn syrup and water. Stir into melted semisweet chocolate until smooth. Beat in coffee and egg yolks one at a time. Fold in cream (Rich Whip) and vanilla. Pour into cooled meringue shell. Chill well.

Bavarian Cream Pie

Try this for a special treat.

> 2 tbsp. milk-free margarine
> ¾ c. sugar
> 2 c. Coffee Rich or milk substitute
> 2 egg yolks, slightly beaten
> 2 bananas, sliced
> ¼ c. cornstarch
> ½ tsp. salt
> 1 tsp. vanilla
> 1 baked pie crust (milk-free)

Melt milk-free margarine. Blend in cornstarch, sugar and salt. Gradually add milk substitute. Heat to boiling over direct heat. Stir into slightly beaten egg yolks. Return to heat and cook 2 minutes, stirring constantly. Add vanilla. Cool thoroughly. Makes 2 cups. Slice bananas and fold into mixture. Add to pie crust. Cover with 2-3 egg meringue if desired (recipe elsewhere in cookbook), or with whipped topping.

VARIATIONS: Use 1 cup coconut to replace bananas or use 1 can Nesselrode mixture to replace bananas.

CHAPTER 14

BEVERAGES

M ANY FRUIT BEVERAGES and carbonated beverages are on the market, so only a few milk substitutes are included here.

Flavorings for Soya Bean Milk*

To improve the flavor of soya milk, one or more of the following may be added (to one cup):

1 tbsp. molasses
1 tbsp. honey
2 tbsp. fruit syrup
2 tbsp. malt syrup
bananas blended in
1 pinch salt
¾ c. frozen raspberries
2 tbsp. maple syrup
2 tsp. vanilla
Chocolate syrup to taste

Orange Frost

¼ c. soya bean milk, undiluted
¼ c. cold water
½ c. orange juice
½ c. crushed ice
1 tbsp. sugar
1 tsp. lemon juice

Combine all ingredients in shaker with tight-fitting lid. Cover and shake well. Serve at once.

---

*Reprinted with permission from Allergy Information Association, Weston, Ontario, Canada.

Rich Cocoa*

4-6 tbsp. cocoa
¼ c. water
½ c. sugar
1 qt. Coffee Rich

Blend cocoa, sugar and water to a smooth paste. Place Coffee Rich into saucepan. Stir in cocoa mixture. Heat but do not boil. Serve with garnish. Yield: 4 servings. Preparation time: 5 minutes. (For an interesting variation add 1 quart of hot black coffee and a dash of cinnamon.)

---

*Reprinted with permission from Rich Products Corp., P.O. Box 245, 1145 Niagara, Buffalo, N.Y.

CHAPTER 15

SOYBEAN RECIPES

Soybean recipes have long been used in oriental cooking. Recently I tried some fresh bean cake from an oriental supply store. It is also called bean curd or Tofu, or soy cheese. This can be used in some ways as a cheese substitute. It is available fresh or canned, but I prefer the fresh. After some experimenting with it I have enclosed a few recipes for its use. If you are interested in experimenting with it I recommend the *Soybean Cookbook* by Mildred Lager and Dorothea Van Gundy Jones and published originally by Devin Adair Co., Old Greenwich, Conn. 06870 and in paperback by ARC Books, Inc., New York, N.Y.

See also Eggless Mayonnaise in Salad section and Beverages.

Bean Cake Dips (Soy Cheese or Tofu)

In a blender add:

> soy cheese (wiped dry)
> ½ tsp. Worcestershire sauce
> Coffee Rich to moisten

Flavor with any of the following:

> bacon bits and 1 or 2 tsp. horseradish
> bacon and onion dip mix
> onion soup mix
> chopped nuts
> chopped bologna and pickle relish
> chopped ham, pimento and pickle relish
> small cocktail sausages
> olives and pimentos, chopped
> chopped shrimp and 1 tsp. lemon juice

Scalloped Soy Cheese and Onions*

diced onions
bread crumbs (milk-free)
canned soy cheese
cream substitute or soy milk

Place a layer of diced onions in a buttered casserole: cover with a layer of canned soy cheese and a few bread crumbs. Alternate onions and cheese until casserole is full. Add a small amount of cream substitute or soy milk and top with bread crumbs. Cover and bake in a moderate oven until done. This is delicious when seasoned with soy sauce.

Soy Cheese Salad and Sandwich Spread*

2 c. soy cheese (fresh, steamed or canned), mashed
¼ c. parsley, chopped
¼ c. celery, chopped
¼ c. chopped olives
2 tbsp. mayonnaise
2 pimentos, chopped

Mix thoroughly and serve cold. Use as sandwich filling or as a salad. Put in center of a tomato cut into fourths and spread open or on tomato slices. Make sandwich of 2 tomato slices with this between, or use 2 pineapple slices with soy cheese salad between them. Serves 2 to 3.

---

*Reprinted with permission from Mildred Lager and Dorothea Jones, *The Soybean Cookbook* (Old Greenwich, Devin-Adair Co., 1963).
*Reprinted with permission from Mildred Lager and Dorothea Jones, *The Soybean Cookbook* (Old Greenwich, Devin-Adair Co., 1963).

Potato Soy Cheese Salad

2 c. boiled potatoes, chopped
1 c. soy cheese
1 lg. cucumber diced
½ c. celery, chopped
mayonnaise

Mix potatoes, cheese, celery and cucumber with mayonnaise. Serve on lettuce-lined salad platter and decorate with radish roses. Serves 4.

Eggless Mayonnaise or Salad Dressing

Soy Cheese Salad Dressing

(*See page 103*)

---

*Reprinted with permission from Mildred Lager and Dorothea Jones, *The Soybean Cookbook* (Old Greenwich, Devin-Adair Co., 1963).

CHAPTER 16

MILK-FREE COMMERCIAL PRODUCTS

A<small>S OF THIS DATE</small> the following products that I have used recently contain no milk or milk products. *However,* remember that the manufacturer may change ingredients at any time, so be sure to check the ingredients over and over.

In my experience, products that contained no milk for long periods of time have suddenly listed a milk product such as non-fat dry milk in the fine print or vice versa, in products that have had milk in the ingredients for years have suddenly dropped it.

Therefore, I cannot guarantee that any of these products will be milk-free when the reader purchases them. I can only state that they were when last I purchased them.

Milk-Free Products

Available at most grocery stores. Remember milk is often listed as whey, casein or sodium caseinate in product ingredients.

Breads and Rolls

Wonder Raisin Rounds®
Hostess
    Scones®
Millbrook
    Italian
    Dutch Dill®
    Pumpernickel Rye®
    Swedish Rye®
Wonder—
    Golden Wheat Bread® or 100% Whole Wheat
    English Muffins
    Raisin Rounds®
Pillsbury Banana Bread Mix®

Stroehman—Hillbilly Bread
Stella Dora—Bread Sticks
    Bread Sticks
    Sesame Bread Sticks
    Pastry Shells
Betty Crocker—Corn Muffin, Wild Blueberry Muffin Mix
Jiffy—
    Honey Date Muffin Mix®
    Blueberry Muffin Mix®
Arnold—Hot dog rolls, sandwich buns, English muffins
Star Market
    Cracked Wheat
    DiPaola® Italian
Most Rye Bread
A & P Cracked Wheat Bread®

Breakfast Foods

Bacon
Sausage
Cereal with milk substitute
Toast with milk-free bread
French toast of Coffee Rich, egg, milk-free bread
Pancakes as below
Bordens Instant Breakfast Drink®

Butter Substitutes

Mazola Unsalted Margarine®
Diet Imperial®
Diet Fleishman's®
Blue Bonnet Diet Margarine®
Spry® or Crisco
Mazola Oil®
Safflower Oil®
Wesson Oil®
Hollywood Safflower Margarine

Cakes

Lady fingers
Angel food—any mix
Applesauce raisin—Duncan Hines®
Lemon Supreme Deluxe II—Duncan Hines & Orange Supreme II
Gingerbread-Pillsbury, Betty Crocker
Some fruit cakes—Dromedary®
Deluxe II Fudge Marble—Duncan Hines®
Deluxe II Banana Supreme—Duncan Hines®
Deluxe II Devils Food—Duncan Hines®   } (Read ingredients
Deluxe II Yellow Cake Mix—Duncan Hines®   } due to recent chang◄
Deluxe II Spice Cake Mix

Candy (hard category, read ingredients)

marshmallows (read label, some brands are okay)
most hard candies (read fine print)
most gum drops
Mounds bars

Casserole Toppings

Cornflake crumbs
Bacon bits
Beancake (or Tofu) bits

Cereals (Serve with milk-substitute, sugar, syrup)

Total®
Rice Krispies, puffed rice and puffed wheat
Oatmeal, Cream of Wheat®, etc.
Special K®
    and most others—hot, cold, instant

Coffee Cakes, Etc.

Aunt Jemima's Coffee Cake Easy Mix®

Pillsbury-Blueberry Coffee Cake Mix®
    Cinnamon Struesel Coffee Cake®
    Apple Cinnamon Coffee Cake Mix®

Cheese Substitutes

Chinese bean cake or soy cheese
Japanese tofu

Cookies

Stella Dora® products (many are milk-free)
Carousel Cremes®—Loblaws
Gingermen®—Pepperidge Farm
Molasses—Pepperidge Farm
Oatmeal—Pepperidge Farm
Lemon Cremes®—Keebler
French Vanilla®—Keebler
Dutch Apple®—Keebler
Old Fashion Oatmeal®—Keebler
Oyster Crackers®—Keebler
Pecan Sandies®—Keebler
Zesta® Saltines—Keebler
Waldorf® Salt Free Crackers—Keebler
Town House® Crackers—Keebler
Sugar Giants®—Keebler
Stars®—Keebler
Rye Toast®—Keebler
Sea Toast®—Keebler
Sesame Bread Wafers®—Keebler
Danish Almond Crescents®—ABC
Pecan Bars®—Pillsbury
Brownie Mix—Pillsbury, Betty Crocker
Double Fudge Brownie Mix®—Duncan Hines
Chocolate Covered Graham (some—read label)
Nabisco—ginger snaps, iced oatmeal raisin cookies, chocolate
chip, coffeebreak cookies

Crackers etc.

Premium® Saltines
Rye Toast®
Ritz
Triscuit®
Triangle Thins®
Sesame Toasts®
Rye Wafers®
Sociables®
Waverly Wafers®
Wheat Thins®

Croutons

Masters
Brownberry—Onion Rye®
Arnold—Onion-Rye Croutons®

Desserts

Italian Ices-not spumoni
Mountain View Frozen Pies®—apple, blueberry, cherry
Any gelatin without whipped cream
Blueberry crisp
Apple Crisp
Cherry crisp
Royal® pudding and pie filling made with milk substitute
Fruit Float®—Libby—with milk substitute
Popsicles®
some JellO pudding mixes (use milk substitute)

Dessert Toppings (See also Whipped Toppings)

Marshmallow creme
Pecans
Strawberry
Pineapple
Walnut
Raspberry (melba)

Gravy

French's Mushroom Gravy Mix®, Onion gravy mix®, Aujus®
Icing –Pillsbury's Fluffy White Frosting Mix®

Lunch Foods

Sandwiches with rye bread (any other milk-free bread)—tuna, ham, chicken, cold meat, hamburger, bacon, bologna (all-beef, milk-free kind), cold cuts (those that contain no milk, whey, caseinate), potato salad, potato chips, baked beans, Heinz® vegetarian beans in tomato sauce
All relishes—pickles, celery, etc. ketchup, chili sauce
Peanut Butter with or without Jelly
Hot dogs—kosher hot dogs, all-beef, Campbell's Beans and Franks®
Minute® rice

Milk and Cream Substitutes

Soybean milks
Mocha mix
Coffee Rich (beware of other brands)

Miscellanous Snacks

Fruit
Pretzels *(read labels—most are milk-free)* Schulers, Snyder's, Bachman
Peanuts, etc.
Potato chips, pop corn (make it)
Slim Jim Beef Snacks®
Fritos®, Doritos®

Pancake Mix

Pillsbury Extra Light®
Pillsbury Blueberry Pancake®

Salad Dressings—Milk-Free

Most French and Italian Dressings, Maries Creamy French®, Chef's Italian®, Kraft's Thousand Island®, Good Seasons® (in envelopes) onion I, Italian, Old-Fashioned French, Garlic, Pfieffer Thousand Island®, Hellman's Mayonnaise®, Wishbone's California Onion Dressing®, Good Seasons Open Pit® Barbecue Sauce and others

Spaghetti Sauce—Cheese Free

Chef Boy-ar-Dee Spaghetti Sauce w/Ground Beef®, Bravo® Spaghetti Sauce—meatless, Conte® Spaghetti sauce, Ragu-Marinara Sauce®

Soups (hard category, read ingredients)

Campbell's—Chicken Rice, Chicken Noodle, Beef Noodle, Chicken Vegetable, Beef Bouillon, Consommé, Vegetarian Vegetable®, Chicken Gumbo®, Curly Noodle®, Noodles and Ground Beef®, Chicken Noodle-O's®: Lipton's Cup-a-Soup®, Beef Noodle, Vegetable (most others contain milk or milk products): Campbell's—Chicken Alphabet, Meatball Alphabet.

Whipped Toppings

Rich's Whipped Topping (aerosol)
Rich Whip Topping—frozen carton
Marshmallow basic-see recipe.

INDEX